To: Mrs. L. Lewis,

May this book inspire
and bless your ministry.

Blessings,

Trudie Reed

The Caring Community

A Journey Into the Spiritual Domain of Transformative Leadership

TRUDIE KIBBE REED, ED.D.

Editor

Claudette McFadden, PhD

iUniverse, Inc.
New York   Bloomington

iUniverse books may be ordered through booksellers or by contacting:

iUniverse
1663 Liberty Drive
Bloomington, IN 47403
www.iuniverse.com
1-800-Authors (1-800-288-4677)

ISBN: 978-1-4401-7047-8 (sc)
ISBN: 978-1-4401-7048-5 (ebook)

Printed in the United States of America

iUniverse rev. date: 01/12/2010

INTERNATIONAL CARING COMMUNITY COLLABORATORY PORT ORANGE

*This book is dedicated to
my husband Ed*

For his love and faith in me

I am forever grateful!

*In deep appreciation
to
my mother,
Rebecca L. Foley*

Contents

Acknowledgments

I wish to acknowledge with deep appreciation the memory of my grandmother, Nana, for her caretaking and nurturing during my formative years and for her support and participation in the endowed caring community that reared me.

I am most grateful to my older brother, Olin, for also nurturing me through my years in the endowed caring community and serving as my guide and protector. I am grateful to Dr. Mary McLeod Bethune, to whom I owe a deep level of gratitude for building a "model community" that continues to showcase the value of caretaking. I wish to thank our trustees, alumni, faculty, staff, students, and our past three university presidents: Dr. James Colston, Dr. Richard V. Moore, and Dr. Oswald P. Bronson Sr., for continuing our founder's legacy and for entrusting the mantle of leadership to me.

I especially wish to thank my husband, Ed, who serves as a voice of reason, logic, and wisdom in support of my work, and for my sons, Jason Preciphs and Joseph Preciphs, for their unconditional love. I also thank my two office enablers, Ashley Johnson, for her graphic designs and illustrations in the book, and Vonshelle Beneby, for serving as a strong advocate and coordinator of the project.

My very special appreciation and thanksgiving for Dr. Claudette McFadden, who is a faithful and spiritual colleague. My appreciation to Dr. Sarah R. Williams, for her generous support in this undertaking, and of course to our very first Dean of the Master's Program in Transformative Leadership, Dr. Anne McCulloch.

I am truly indebted to The United Methodist Church for my many years of education, training, and nurturing that spans for three decades, and especially, for the practical experience of how to build caring communities through my work as general secretariat of the General Commission on the Status and Role of Women.

This book would not have been possible without the faith shown in me by Dr. Norman E. Dewire, former General Secretary of the General Council on Ministries, who challenged me to attend graduate school and then ensured that it became a reality. I owe my gratitude to my dear mentor, Dr. Elizabeth Kasl, who embraced me during my doctoral dissertation at Teacher's College, Columbia University, and stimulated my inquiry into collaborative processes and transformative learning.

I wish to thank my current Board of Trustees' Chairperson, Dr. Irving Matthews, and also the Bahamas Conference of the Methodist Church for inspiring me to finally sit down to write this book.

Ultimately, my humble thanksgiving is to God for the blessing of serving as the fifth president of the *GREAT* Bethune-Cookman University!

Preface

During my early thirties, while serving as an administrator within my church denomination, I was assigned the role of coordinating a nationwide coalition that would build and strengthen rural and small-town congregations. A gathering of national ministers and laity was planned and implemented by those who served and led these kinds of congregations. My experience was primarily from inner-city ministries, so I was virtually unaware of the real issues and struggles confronting this constituency group.

As soon as I arrived at the conference registration table, I felt tension and mistrust. I attributed this initial feeling of uneasiness to being viewed as an outsider who did not belong. This feeling appeared to be confirmed because few people acknowledged my presence. I convinced myself this was just another meeting to which I was assigned. After all, my charge was to collaborate with two other key staff administrators who happened to be the *real experts* in the area of ministries in rural and small-town congregations. Nevertheless, I accepted my position and role as the *figure-head* leader who was present primarily to carry out a four-year assigned study process on behalf of the denomination.

It certainly did not alleviate my discomfort to see that there was only one other African American person present and one Latino man from the East Coast. My inner being told me that my talents were not desired by this constituency group. What I could not have guessed at the time was that *every person there had the same sense of disempowerment I was experiencing.*

As I reflect back to the first day of the conference, signs of mistrust and victim behavior were evident as I observed members of the group blaming others for individual and group failure. With almost one hundred attendees present, I rejoiced over not having to play a major leadership role. Just imagine my surprise when I was asked by the other two administrators to facilitate a discussion session around cluster groups that had visited various local rural and small-church congregations that Sunday morning. Since I was a fairly seasoned group facilitator, it sounded like something I could do. I told myself this role was rather benign and okay for me to accept.

Around 6 PM, I assumed the facilitator role and started the group session with a prayer, followed by brief instructions on the group reporting process. With newsprint and colored markers in hand, I was fully energized to capture the themes that surely would emerge and so, I started to call for cluster group presentations with a sense of excitement. Without any warning, the entire group suddenly exploded when a white pastor (referred to as Sam) and the sole Latino man in the group (referred to as Daniel) entered into a serious verbal conflict. Daniel had displayed rather aggressive behavior and managed to irritate almost all of us from the moment we met him. We soon learned that Sam had sarcastically referred to Daniel as "Peppy," and the unacceptable name-calling precipitated a rather serious conflict between the two. Voices escalated, and the threat of physical violence ensued. We learned that Daniel saw being called "out of his name" as a threat to his masculinity. So there I stood, in charge, praying silently to God for every bit of wisdom and every ounce of facilitator training I had ever received just to get the group through this terrible ordeal.

As I attempted to have Sam and Daniel dissect their conflict by describing why and how it had developed, others in the room began to speak of their hurt and distrust of other races of people; raw experiences from respective congregations; illustrations pointing to low self-esteem; and anger against one particular bishop back home because of a perceived insult. Suddenly, it was clear that the process was out of control. It was also clear that I did not have a clue about how to get back on track.

The room felt like a popcorn machine popping without its lid; popcorn flew across the room without regard to where it landed. Almost everyone in the plenary room managed to retrieve and recount past negative treatments or hurts. Many began just to blurt out examples. The gathering had literally turned into a group therapy session where, on one side of the room, physical violence awaited, and on the other side, hurt and angry experiences filled the remaining meeting space.

Only later did I understand what I was really witnessing: *a noncaring community at its very worst.* Yet I was being challenged to transform it on the spot! Noncaring communities are exceedingly dangerous, and if left alone, they are also capable of destroying the very fabric of an existing foundation, not to mention the organizational mission.

It was almost midnight before I was able to bring closure to the chaos and the nightmare that had erupted before my very eyes. I wisely used my time as the facilitator by slowly allowing stories to be told and having each person identify his/her common experiences with similar hurts and grief that had been stored for too long in the hearts and minds of participants. Yet I was also grateful for a new awareness. It was the awareness that the tension I had first perceived was not the result of differences of race, gender, experience, or even church size. I had been wrong.

We shared of ourselves and wept together until around midnight, and as there was only a pitcher of water and a bowl of fruit left in the room, we used those items for the blood and body of Jesus Christ and had Communion. I observed many healing moments, and only one person in the group refused to participate in this act of reconciliation. When I saw Sam and Daniel embrace after communion, my heart was warmed.

After having Communion, I realized we were on the brink of laying a foundation that could eventually lead to the formation of a caring and nurturing community. Only then would we really be able to collectively look beyond our brokenness and untested assumptions to work in unity in order to achieve a common mission and have productive work sessions.

Our group suffered conflict because we did not take the necessary time to adequately build and nurture one another into a collective body. While there had been an earlier short session that attempted community building, the process was incomplete as the group rushed too quickly into tasks and work. First it was necessary to establish trust for the building of a cohesive team. We needed to get to know each other's stories, personal journeys, and gifts. By failing to observe our individual and collective gifts, we could not dream together. Nor could we attend to the business at hand. Because we each arrived with various untested assumptions, we acted out of our fears and self-doubts. Without initially establishing caretaking practices as our group covenant, participants unwittingly opted to focus on our vulnerabilities, which ended up serving as the curriculum for our time together. We placed our collective negative energy into isolated pockets of fear, which quickly contaminated our processes.

I had initially assumed that the group was cohesive, especially since participants shared a common purpose and mission around the rural church. I could not have been more wrong. A shared commonality of experience, or even a shared mission, does not equal or ensure a Caring Community. This false assumption is a common mistake made by many organizational leaders and their partners/collaborators. While church groups may desire to follow corporate meeting styles, which forego community building, I discovered that the church either consciously or unconsciously claims our Christian heritage of connectedness and community. When churches attempt to employ the corporate models of leadership, there is often resentment. I suspect that the resentment has its roots in the expectation that engagement will in fact be modeled after Christ and his disciples. Consciously, when we do not pay attention to the need to establish a nurturing environment within our respective churches, congregational leaders encounter greater difficulty in fostering revitalization within their churches.

Reflecting back to my conference experience on rural life ministries, it seemed impossible that any plans, programs, or improvements for outreach ministries would have met with success, for insomuch as our own leadership team had not been formed. Looking back, what is now apparent is that uncaring communities inhibit vision, change, or discernment for both personal and organizational growth. This dysfunctional group was too fragmented and conflicted to be productive in any respect.

When we examine effective and productive organizations, stakeholders are aligned with a common mission and purpose. We also find unity and harmony toward a vision and people who are motivated and genuinely excited. Within highly effective organizations, organizational leaders focus on building a strong community in order to attend to the work and tasks at hand.

The story of the rural church illustrates the value and need for nurturing communities, especially when we strive to empower self and others. Caring Communities can be established for both shorter or longer intervals, for the purpose of conducting inquiries into meaning or to test ideas for our present and future. Essentially, once the community bonding takes shape, the community of participants will find ways to remain connected long past the meeting or conference. This is how powerful and important these nurturing communities can become. Caring Communities can become formalized, as in the case of an ongoing and continuous meeting group such as the Group for Collaborative Inquiry. They may also result in a collective force or mindset of goodwill that guides ongoing reflection. My Endowed Caring Community from my neighbor of elders that held meetings with us is an example of a collective mindset.

Later in the book, you will come to understand how my elders guided my value formation, my decision-making, and my self-critique. Although the majority of the members of my Endowed Caring Community are now deceased, they continue to enable me to engage in critique, evaluation of perspectives, and challenges toward new insights. These elder community leaders give voice to my need to continually be involved in other communities that will assist me in exploration and inquiry.

Focus Of This Book

The *primary premise of the book* is that **Caring Communities** are needed for they serve an important role in the process of bonding groups of individuals for the purpose of productive work, processing ideas, and for our survival. Caring Communities are a prerequisite for transformative leadership. Caring Communities serve as the vehicle and catalyst for framing issues, for critical reflectivity, group and individual visioning, and even for the discernment that is necessary for lasting transformation.

The role of Caring Communities is to facilitate our seeking and searching for the "truth," through a systematic review of traditions and habits that lock us into static thinking and behavior patterns. The systematic review process from the Caring Community begins our own internal review, which is ongoing and continuous both inside and outside of the Community. It must be clarified that the use of the term "transformation" does not automatically ensure that individuals or their organizations will change. The term "transformative leadership" is used to convey a process of facilitation whereby the community group remains focused on the critique of ideas and assumptions that inform our decision-making. The primary goal of transformative leadership is to provide, through facilitation, an opportunity for our participation in a continuous learning process whereby individuals engage in a review of mental models and paradigms through a praxis of dialogue, critique, and reflection. The systematic process of critical thinking can be facilitated by any or all members of a particular community, or by an outside consultant.

Because nurturing communities drive the transformative process of learning, organizations must have the establishment and sustaining of Caring Communities as their foundation. These communities become safe havens for ideas and innovation.

For organizations that desire change, the engagement of Caring Communities, both intellectually and emotionally, provides the leadership context for revitalization. For each organization of every category and type to become vital, viable, and relevant for the postmodern age in which we live, transformational processes must be a part of organizational culture.

The *second premise* is that Caring Communities can provide a lens into the affective domain, where organizations and their leaders are able to activate the spiritual dimension of leadership. The affective domain, also referred to as the *spiritual domain*, is a sacred place where ideas are born; where new meaning is derived; where visions form new realities; where we become personally transformed; and where discernment from God becomes manifest. In moving to the spiritual domain of learning, *discernment* is often possible for seeking the will of God. When this occurs, many individuals are dramatically transformed in both their thinking and actions. Many church leaders speak of discernment as a gift from God. The manifestation of discernment is a powerful force that moves many people to the places they least expected to be. Many church leaders speak of discernment and movement of the Holy Spirit as a conversion experience. I believe everyone has an opportunity to receive this gift as I have experienced it through my participation in Caring Communities. Even when we are unable to discern, the process of transformation is still a powerful educational tool in and of itself.

Caring Communities have all but vanished in many parts of our nation, yet we are dependent on them to ensure that our directions and perspectives are reviewed, studied, and critiqued. However, as each chapter of this book unfolds, you will travel on a journey through my personal transformation with stories about the value of such communities. The stories recounted in this book are intended to guide your discussions of how your organizations can explore, and perhaps even cross into, the *spiritual domain* of learning and leading.

The Caring Community: A Journey into the Spiritual Domain of Transformative Leadership is a necessary read for every woman and man of God who has determined that the church must assume its rightful leadership role as a change agent in a world outside of the will of God. Very simply, its goal is the revitalization of *both* faith and secular communities, which can only be accomplished through minds that are made transformative. It is time that we become the change we have prayed to God for. This journey is designed just for you and your organization. *Dare you travel along an uncharted path ... to glimpse a vision of your future?*

Introduction

My Survival Through A Caring Community

During my early twenties, I worked for a large state university in the early 1970s that was attempting to attract more minority students. As an African American entry-level employee, working in the student affairs sector, my job was to elicit cooperation from counselors across the state in support of our mandate to increase the number of minority students applying and, ultimately, matriculating at our institution. Unfortunately, my university employer had earned a negative reputation for not being very hospitable to people of color. While espousing change, the organizational actions were just the opposite. It was most difficult to succeed, but I was determined!

In addition to working to increase the number of enrolled minority students, my position also included facilitating the university's efforts to embrace diversity through program development and shifts in both mindset and actions for professional employees and students across the campus. Each of these goals was of particular interest to me inasmuch as the university was also my alma mater.

I vividly remember what it was like being one of only one hundred African American students, from 1966 to 1970, in the University of Texas's 40,000-plus student body. I am certain that I only survived this horrible period and many of the experiences associated with it because of the anchor created by my upbringing within a Caring Community.

As I reflect on being called ugly names, being denied service at various restaurants, and getting barred from on-campus female housing, I understand today what I did not understand then: namely, my journey of transformation was never intended to be easy, just as it was not easy for the early church, which endured harsh persecution and criticism by the religious elite of its day. Moreover, the journey's beginning would be fraught with obstacles and barriers stacked high and deep ... with odds for success attainable only by those who were steadfast and determined. I am pleased to recall that all one hundred African American students formed a strong bond and supportive community that enabled us to survive. Our strongly bonded community sustained each of us right through graduation. We frequently gathered together, prayed together, shared together, cried together, reflected together, critiqued together, studied together, questioned together, and strategized together as we tried to make sense of an experience that felt like a war zone. We learned as much in our Caring Community as we did in our course subjects. The lessons learned were lifelong and transformative. Our success at staying the course resulted from our personal transformation, which was facilitated within our cohort group where we derived nurture and unconditional acceptance in our Caring Community.

My Introduction to Transformational Leadership

I also recall that as an employee of my alma mater in the early 1970s, I developed and then later implemented a series of workshops and skill-training events that were intended to provide assistance and support to university leaders in their development of cultural awareness and sensitivity, especially where African American students were concerned. Although we attempted many approaches to consciousness awareness and racial inclusiveness, nothing appeared to work. In the face of facts and sound reasoning, I was perplexed as I tried to understand why senior leaders still had difficulty understanding the plight and needs of African American students on their respective campuses. I actually remember reaching a point where I just gave up on society and most of its leaders. My experiences had led me to conclude that nothing and no one would ever be able to affect change in the belief systems of those who held power—those who had categorically refused to change!

It was not until I approached the ripe age of forty that I was first introduced to transformative learning in my graduate studies. It was only then that my thinking about change, as a process, was confronted. Little did I realize that I had actually left the conventional world of thinking and was entering a doorway that would catapult me into a world of transformative thinking and transformative leading.

Long before the language of "transformative leadership" was popularized, I was engaged in my doctoral research study, where my findings revealed that shifts in behavior are very different than transitions in beliefs and perspectives. I realized that what I had attempted in the 1970s was change in the behavior of others when what I really wanted was to affect transition in value systems. However, the only transformation I experienced was internal—my very own.

In 1987, I conducted research and discovered a powerful connection between changing one's core values and accessing the "affective domain" of learning (touching the heart). I discovered that it was not enough to just foster dialogue, reflection, and critique, as described in my initial study of adult education theory. My research unveiled the role of the spiritual domain in transforming values and beliefs. The spiritual domain, I discovered, is the portal for effecting possible shifts in our perspectives and values. My finding was a radical departure from prior conclusions I held about value transformation, although intuitively, I must have known that transformation was really a spiritual concept and process. Learning that the catalyst for transitions in thinking and beliefs is movement through the affective domain of learning, I also discovered that is where God speaks to us. And when this occurs, our logic gives way to our hearts, where amazing gifts of the Spirit reside.

In all candor, I must say that on the other side of this doorway of discovery, I found few bosses who saw value in the new ideas and new perspectives that attended transformative leading. The paradigm they were most comfortable with was not one in which there was excitement and readiness to embrace me as a visionary leader committed to challenging conventional thinking. However, this is precisely the way I viewed myself. I very quickly came to understand that my life would be lived as a visionary and a transformative leader. In my mind, this was an immutable and undeniable fact.

You should know that my original research into transformative *learning* was conducted solely within The United Methodist Church, with volunteers assigned to the two National United Methodist agencies with mission-related social justice mandates. My target population was those individuals who were originally from annual conferences but whom had subsequent appointments to the national agencies. It is important to qualify the surveyed population by pointing out that the one distinguishing characteristic was that each of these individuals held conservative views on a variety of issues. My specific aim was to observe and document any changes that occurred in their value systems that, subsequently, led to their support and/or acceptance of controversial issues.

The study identified *a significant emotional experience* as the trigger for the radical transformation experienced by once-conservative volunteers. Again, it is important to point out that not everyone who has a significant emotional experience will be changed. Indeed, it is possible for a person to be touched at the level of his or her heart and still not be moved to rethink or reevaluate previously held beliefs, attitudes, or assumptions. It is also possible that the change *does* take immediate effect. Either reflection will be fleeting rather than enduring, or it may be continuous and eventually manifest in transitions of beliefs at a much later time. In the study, all but one person modified his/her traditional perspectives and beliefs. While this is an insightful and intriguing finding, it also spoke to me as the absence of any "universal or guaranteed conversion" associated with accessing the affective domain of learning. An ethical clarification on acts of transformational leadership is that neither leaders nor partners in the process have the right to force change on others. Instead, our role is to create conditions in which people in our organizations and communities may examine those things that may be held dear yet may impede individual and organizational growth.

The majority of my study participants described "significant emotional experiences" that led them to changes in position and ideology; they referred to them as "the Holy Spirit at work." In this way, the overwhelming majority of my study's participants described their own inner change. They were verifying the important role of the "heart." For Christians, we understand this theological characterization because throughout the Gospel, Jesus transformed those who followed him. My research into The United Methodist Church brought important revelations for church members and for me as well. The research is also readily applicable to other organizational settings. This is because the power inherent in accessing the affective domain of learning is present within us all, regardless of organization.

As I analyzed and reflected on my research findings, I concluded that the affective domain of learning was unconsciously being used by and within agencies that had little, if any, conscious knowledge that learning at this important level was taking place. While my agency's personnel freely utilized storytelling and shared life experiences as a part of their regular meeting format for group bonding, these same individuals seemed oblivious to the significant emotional impact that telling stories and sharing personal experiences had on their volunteers. Through storytelling and sharing personal experiences, agency personnel unwittingly accessed the affective domain and, in so doing, ushered in a change within their volunteers—a change that resulted in much deeper levels of caring and, like the Apostle Paul, new ways of thinking and acting. Without realizing it, through the use of stories and personal experiences, agency personnel had reached their volunteers' hearts and, in doing so, had changed some of their core beliefs and values. What became clearer over time was that within these two study sites of my research project, Caring Communities had been formed that facilitated deep inner and community reflection, a nurturing and trusting community, and dramatic shifts in perspectives among members.

Now, as president of a major historically black university located within the heart of a community that I now call my home and an ever-watchful analyst of the times in which we live, I know there is a need for the development of leadership both within and outside of the academy. The cultural context in which students have grown up; men, women, and children have worked and worshipped; and businesses have operated is marked by rapid societal change which, quite literally, can cause one's head to spin. Change is readily evident through technological, social, global, political, and economic shifts that impact organizations (clergypeople, educators, and business men and women). Concurrent with these changes is an accelerating work pace that is driven by a communications and an information explosion unlike anything we have seen at any other time. New fusions of regional cultures throughout the world; increasing interaction of people from various social, racial, and ethnic backgrounds as a direct outgrowth of advances in transportation technologies; global marketplaces where historical divisions are becoming increasingly irrelevant; and both the natural and crisis migrations of people go far in supporting Thomas Friedman's supposition that the "world is flat" (Freidman 2005). Needless to say, profound ethical shifts are concomitant with these and many other twenty-first century developments. Understandably, organizations (e.g., churches, schools, and businesses) throughout the world are directing their energies toward these and other developments and changes.

I have become convinced that change must be driven by communities which are ethically centered and care about others. Within these nurturing communities, we must find balance as a response to the rapidly changing society that is causing us to be more reactive than proactive. Caring Communities focus on individual and collective values and, thereby, ensure reflective and prayerful change in religious communities, educational institutions, and businesses. Unlike the two organizations in my study that unconsciously employed elements of transformative leadership, Caring Communities must be deliberate in their roles and the application of *transformative leadership.*

There is no question that my research findings represented a marked departure from conventional wisdom, which maintained that, if organizations and experts had data that had been generated through empirical research, they would have everything that was needed to prepare individuals for effective work and service within their various churches, schools, and businesses.

In former times, deficits in this area were met through the development and utilization of skills-based workshops and sound management alone, aimed specifically at leaders in business, government, and higher education. Church leadership was virtually invisible as sponsors of and much less participants in these skills-based workshops. These workshops were predicated on behavioral models that transmitted information and skills on such topics as diversity, race, gender, and age inclusion and came as society struggled to enter a doorway marked "Affirmative Action," a policy mandated by the laws of our nation.

Year after year, American educational and leadership programs continued to be challenged as a direct result of diversity initiated by a governmental policy that forced individuals to explore new paradigms. The failure of Affirmative Action has its roots in the fact that neither government nor nongovernmental organizations effectively facilitated the transition that was needed to appropriately address pervasive faulty assumptions about race and gender that were so prevalent within the workforce. The unfortunate result was a continuation of negative stereotypes, biases, and resentment toward diversity and, by default, Affirmative Action. Responses came nowhere near transformative learning and those individuals who led workshops, seminars, and seminar responses were far from being transformative thinkers and leaders.

The truth is that, even in the face of seminars and skills-based workshops, Affirmative Action represented a major cognitive and moral challenge for America's dominant culture from one coast to the other. The ability to don a different pair of lenses in order to see things differently was a completely foreign notion. Long-held assumptions and traditional ways of addressing issues were too familiar. The tried and tested ways, even though not necessarily successful, were just safer. Sadly, the consequence of being unwilling to look beyond the status quo is always a workplace environment that is plagued by ongoing conflicts and misunderstandings because the mindsets of the men and women who exercise power and, as a consequence, those they lead, remain static. Affirmative Action failed as a forced change because it required more than behavior shifts. The human heart (spiritual domain) was required for testing possible shifts in the values and beliefs of those who resisted the change.

Many organizational leaders admitted that being confronted with directives to diversify and/or accept diversity in the workplace was difficult for them because neither ownership nor understanding attended their efforts to comply. Moreover, organizational leaders lacked educational processes that would enable them to expand or shift the mindsets of the great majority of white Americans who held positions of power and influence. A significant number of white Americans felt that, rather than qualifications, color and race had become the primary factors whenever decisions were made that moved them out of a position and African Americans into the position. More importantly, these leaders never got to know minorities on a human level. Since the Caring Community model serves as a catalytic agent for bonding and embracing change that is sincere and from the heart, it is the only way that value shifts would have become manifest.

Suddenly, all of my experiences became clearer. I now understood that my journey through my alma mater and the survival of that hostile experience served to reinforce the importance of the Caring Community I had participated in on campus. Conversely, the hostility that I experienced with the rural life ministry group was due to the lack of a nurturing environment. From these two experiences, I concluded the important role of Caring Communities and their ability to transform negative energy into positive outcomes. I further realized that all of my hard work on preparing skill workshops had been in vain. My journey on the pathway of transformational leadership was just beginning, and I loved it!

Several definitions are offered for understanding and clarity about the transformative leadership process that serves as a catalytic agent for change, as well as the vehicle that is capable of transporting us to the doorway of spiritual domain. The definition of Caring Communities further supports their important role as the foundation for learning processes that equip us with necessary tools for re-examination of assumptions and for needed individual and organizational change.

Definitions

Transformative Leadership is the "art and science" of facilitating value-centered change or movement through a review of assumptions and beliefs held by both the individual and organization. Within this process, the Community engages group dialogue in which the focus is on a critique of assumptions held by individuals and their organization. Within this continuous process of dialogue and reflection, participants critique their reality and may activate the spiritual domain where visioning and **discernment** are made possible. This transformative process of learning and discovery enables leaders and their collaborative partners to vision what is not presently known or seen.

The **spiritual domain**, also referred to as the affective domain of learning, is where feelings overshadow logic long enough for the creation of a learning space that produces deeper reflection and radical change. Within the Christian community, we often describe this learning space as the Holy Spirit intervening in our midst. It is a moment in time when God speaks to our hearts and we are moved to some form of new action. The spiritual domain does not allow logic and left-brain reasoning processes to block the movement of discernment. **Discernment** is defined as an act by which God speaks to us through our hearts and soul. Similarly, Christian laity and clergy understand conversion experiences where people are powerfully motivated to proclaim Jesus Christ as central to their lives, even if they have not been previously a part of any church or faith group.

Visioning is the gift of dreaming within a safe and nurturing cohort of transformative minded individuals, or it can also occur as a result of discernment. Many times we hear of a visionary leader who is able to dream new realities because their leadership lens is tuned into reflective practice. Or, some such leaders actually have a gift of discernment through yielding their will to the will of God—by listening—by reflecting—by praying—by waiting—by being obedient to their calling. When we are in the present with such leaders and partner/collaborators, we are in awe of the miracles that emerge within our churches and other organizations. You will see that these nurturing Caring Communities may be formed within any organization that has basic humanistic values.

My personal stories that are recounted in this book are intended to demonstrate the influence of both the Caring Community and its ability to enable leaders and followers to access the spiritual domain of learning. You will explore my journey of transformation and the impact my Caring Community had in touching my heart and producing dramatic change in my perspectives, attitudes, and behavior.

Caring Communities are clusters of individuals who are equal in their participation in group dialogue sessions; in making inquiry into new meaning; and their critique of existing realities and individual assumptions. Within these nurturing and sustaining bodies, leaders do not have power over other participants but share equally in discussions. At the moment the leader joins a Caring Community, his/her position and role as leader is minimized. Caring communities create, foster, and sustain effective nurturing environments for the purposes of:

- Building trust among all participants
- Producing group bonding
- Creating a safe place for risk-taking
- Providing nurture to one another
- Framing issues for critique
- Ensuring that decisions and discussions focus on values and ethics
- Transmitting culture, history, and tradition while simultaneously examining needed innovations
- Facilitating open-ended priorities or an agenda beyond serving as a reference group for inquiry into a variety of issues, concerns, and tradition
- Inviting and accepting—unconditional acceptance
- Questioning and probing
- Visioning and discernment

A major mistake many faith-based groups make is thinking that *solidarity* conveys *trust*. This is not always the case. While individuals may work together on a common mission or need, solidarity in action or deeds does not mean that trust is automatic. For example, the notion that solidarity and trust are one in the same is a failure of many social justice movements, and this misconception has led to friction, negative power dynamics, and other dysfunctional behaviors. The essence of the Caring Community concept is to establish trust as the foundation for the most difficult group work of truth telling, self-examination, and critique of the assumptions held by those in the community. Without trust, the competing personal needs of individuals may destroy the efforts of Caring Community and, most certainly, discernment.

If asked how one forms a Caring Community, the answer is to provide several options. While it is desirable for groups no larger than forty-five people to organize just for the purpose of dialogue, bonding, and framing critical social issues, many groups do not begin this way. Normally, groups form around some topic or mandate. Conferences, for example, are topic related and are planned and implemented toward some specific goal or mission. Nevertheless, all groups should begin with the intention of forming a Caring Community as the foundation for its work. Caring Communities must exist to build trust, to examine assumptions, and to collectively discern the will of God.

While it is advisable that Caring Communities originate for the sole purpose of collective sharing, critical reflection, and discernment, this goal may not be realistic, or even possible, within our postmodern society. Caring Communities are process-driven as opposed to task-oriented. However, they can become viable even within a task group if that organization solidly establishes the foundation necessary for moving beyond dialogue to a deeper level of group critique and reflection. In such instances, the emphasis slowly shifts from "tasks" to "community," and it may eventually evolve toward the spiritual dimension of leadership, where discernment is made possible. The solid foundation of a Caring Community means that even after long breaks in organizational settings, the community can reassemble and reclaim momentum. The Caring Community is self-sustaining and creates a lasting effect.

A conceptual view of the role of Caring Communities and the Transformative Leadership Process is described below in **Figure 1**

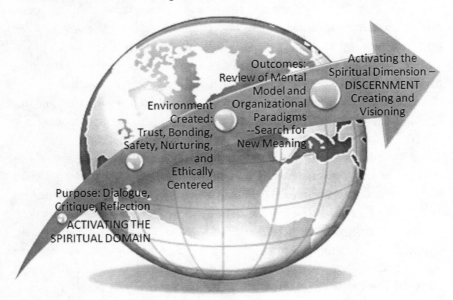

Members of Caring Communities demonstrate their commitment to this nurturing group through regular attendance, honest feedback, respect for others, and accountability for value-centered behaviors and actions. These nurturing bodies are not only concerned with dialogue, reflection, and critique, but they may also claim a spiritual role of seeking God's wisdom through acts of discernment and visioning. In this sense, Caring Communities are facilitators for transformative leadership.

How Are Caring Communities Different from Other Groups?

Caring Communities differ from other configurations of people or social clubs because they embrace all of humanity by seeking wisdom from a higher source through the convergence of diverse thoughts and ideas. Unlike social clubs, nonprofit agencies, or business agencies, Caring Communities are process-driven and perform without a set agenda or programmatic outcomes. Their curricula or purpose for existing is to examine, vision, question, and listen to one another for new insights. There may not be special purposes for the gathering other than serving one another through these learning processes. It is important to note that while many groups start out with one purpose, they can abandon that original purpose or task, and end up becoming a Caring Community. For these communities to be effective, there must be a balance of power. All people must be fully empowered as equal participants.

When asked whether reading circles, therapy groups, sororities and fraternities, Chautauqua Movements, or even group therapy sessions constitute Caring Communities, my response is predicated on the definition and role of each. For example, I have known some literary and book club groups to build such strong bonds among members that the group will set aside their initial mission of book discussions or publication just to attend to the needs of their newly formed cohort community. I once belonged to a women's literary group called the Group for Collaborative Learning. We initially had a mission of collaborating just for purposes of publication in the field of adult education. After a year of intense work together, and a few publications in academic journals, we were so bonded that the focus on publication became secondary and we eventually met just as a cohesive supportive Caring Community. We challenged theories, concepts, ideas, and made new meaning. We also cared deeply about each other and provided emotional and spiritual support to one another. As I reflect back to that experience, I was nurtured and challenged to grow while participating in that group.

Because Caring Communities and the process of group therapy may both provide growth of some kind to participants, it must be clarified that group therapy is a psycho-dynamic process that is concerned with the individual's psychological well-being whereas Caring Communities have a quite different purpose that may not directly address any psychological problem at hand. Caring Communities may be therapeutic, but that is not their purpose. Social groups and fraternal orders have yet another mission that may invalidate their ability to consistently serve as Caring Communities.

Chapter I:

My Caring Community

When I was only nine years old, during the Jim Crow era, I was angry with all of white America regarding the mistreatment of African Americans. There were segregated schools, water fountains marked "Colored," and many other symbols representative of that separate, unequal, and very terrible time in our nation's history. All too often, I observed African American men and women who could not read or write being taken advantage of by white insurance company agents who entered our communities each Friday to collect burial fees for life insurance policies sold to our elders. My own grandmother, Nana, was one of their clients.

Nana was a domestic worker who earned a living by cleaning homes three days a week and occasionally on Saturdays. Her salary augmented my mother's income and enabled them to feed, house, and clothe us. My mother was a single parent who had the support of Nana and an endowed community. Nana and my mother worked hard and worshiped every Sunday. They made sure we were fed, and Nana provided discipline that, decades later, continues to give meaning to my moral development. Prayer, obedience, and accountability were all the gifts entrusted to us as their children.

If Nana earned fifteen dollars a week, the insurance collector got five. Though only nine, I had excellent reading and reasoning skills, and it was very apparent to me that these policies were never intended to be stamped "Paid in Full." The weekly presence of these insurance men was a constant reminder of the variety of ways in which we were preyed on and disgraced.

Neither my brother nor I was ever able to convince Nana that her insurance payments would never be applied to her burial. Trying to get her to think more critically, I remember asking such questions as, "Nana, what if you placed the funds you pay the insurance man in the bank so you can receive interest?", "Nana, do you really think the policy will pay for anything?", and "Nana, do you think you are being preyed upon?" My grandmother's only response was to smile. One day, however, she revealed to me that she saw no other choice except to place her trust in the insurance agent.

There were times when I overheard the conversations between Nana and her insurance agent. It seemed that, over the years, they had managed to form a collegial relationship, and occasionally my grandmother would discuss spiritual matters with him. She even offered him advice and elder wisdom. Years later, when I thought about those times, I knew that my grandmother was right; she really did not have many other options, especially since she had only a sixth grade education. She accepted an interpretation of information from someone who she believed had her best interest in mind and who also had the necessary expertise. In the absence of better education, most of us would have likely done the same thing.

As I reflect, I think that Nana must have paid a burial fee every week for more than twenty years. As an adult, I never recalled seeing proof of payment or any kind of report on her burial policy. It was and continues to be quite obvious that Nana only represented a paycheck to the insurance collector. If you were to ask my grandmother how she could be so trusting, she would tell you that ultimately her trust was in God, who understood that she was doing her best to care for her family.

Throughout the years of my youth, I observed these insurance collectors coming and going, while all the time preying on an entire community of "kind" and "hard working" men and women who wanted nothing more than to be able to trust the promises that were made to them about burial insurance. My Nana exercised tremendous faith. In fact, in her view, the same faith that had allowed her to trust that God would understand her limitations and her heart was the very same faith that led her to trust the insurance agent who sold her an insurance burial policy. Although there was little that I or my older brother Olin could do to convince Nana that she was being exploited, I pledged that I would never be as vulnerable when it came to placing my trust in others.

My Nana, like the other members of the endowed Caring Community in which I was raised, demonstrated extraordinary love, respect, and care through her daily selfless actions. In my grandmother's thinking, payment of one's burial cost was an important way to show respect to family members who would be faced with myriad challenges following the death of a loved one in general, and their own death in particular. As a perpetual caretaker, my Nana joined countless other community elders whose payments on burial policies were their sincere efforts to remove a predictable and, in their view, completely avoidable burden.

You see, ours was an endowed Caring Community where folks transmitted positive values to the youth through legacy stories, examples of sacrifice, and unconditional acceptance. It was a community where elders shared their faith stories, modeled a positive work ethic, and motivated young people like my brother and me to become educated. The Caring Community that I speak of was filled with hope-givers determined to pass on to its young people a better quality of life. The people were proud and respectable. They worshiped in their respective church each Sunday and gave freely to support the work of the church, even with very limited resources. Every adult worked one or more jobs as both an investment in and sacrifice for the future of the community's young people.

When families or individual members of our endowed Caring Community faced hardships, neighbors and friends stepped up and reached in and, through collections and drives, worked to lessen and even remove the hardship. The words of Kirk Franklin's acclaimed song, "I Need You to Survive," reflect the very spirit that the elders had for my endowed community:

I need you. You need me
We're all a part of God's body
Stand with me, agree with me
We're all a part of God's body

It is his will that every need be supplied
You are important to me
I need you to survive
I'll pray for you
You pray for me
I love you
I need you to survive
I won't harm you
With words from my mouth
I love you
I need you to survive.
(Franklin 2002)

This spirit was ubiquitous and fervently embraced in my Caring Community. My Caring Community refused to let whatever faults its young people might have had outweigh their commitment and resolve to meet our needs. We were the light in their eyes, and this knowledge gave us the confidence to say to every mountain, "Be ye removed."

The members of the endowed Caring Community where I grew up also possessed a strong sense of accountability. Few mothers abandoned their duties as good parents. If one did, she had to face an outraged community of elders who were all too happy to remind her of her responsibility as an adult and as a mother. There was also a sense of shame if any member disrespected others. This was particularly true where our seniors were concerned because we had been given unmistakable values and common sense by our elders, who were, in fact, our moral compasses.

Whenever a young person forgot himself or herself and their within the larger community through a disrespectful word or act, he or she knew at once that the line of acceptable conduct had been crossed. And so, in the seconds that immediately followed the utterance or the act, personal regret was swift, as news of this shameful violation was already being passed on. Siblings of the offender and friends who were present thanked God that this violation of community trust had not been their own. We were ashamed of such conduct in ourselves and genuinely concerned about the shame we would cause our families because we knew we had been raised better, and that mattered to us.

The success that I have experienced in my life was ensured by this endowed African American neighborhood. It was a Dallas, Texas, community where neighbors were my extended family, my educators, and my accountability measure. It was where the elders gave their very best to ensure that the community's youth were grounded in positive values, and we were motivated to become well educated. Their love for us continues to engulf my emotions.

I am the first to admit that this type of neighborhood and community is rarely seen today. It is almost a certainty that few hands would be raised were we to poll congregants in a church body, students in a university classroom, or employees of an industrial complex about whether their growing up experiences mirror my own. The frightening truth is that, as a nation, we have devolved into cities, towns, communities, and neighborhoods full of mean streets and even meaner spirits. Our communities are places where neither the elders nor the babies are protected from hurt, harm, or danger; places where each person has become nearly invisible to the other; places where nobody knows or wants to know your name; places where looking the other way and crossing to the other side is more common than not and can only be called what it is—a shameless conspiracy of silence—places where the Holy Spirit is constantly grieved.

I believe in the power and potential of the endowed Caring Community to do work for God. I believe that the heaven on Earth that Christians so often speak of is ushered in through the birth and spiritual energy that comes from these communities. Finally, I am convinced that the spiritual domain of transformative leadership is divinely connected and attuned to the work that awaits us in the reestablishment of these communities.

Why Are Caring Communities Important?

First and foremost, Caring Communities are "endowed groups" that are bound by common goals that preserve, support, and nurture. They also push toward a critique of traditions and habits that may block creativity and vision. These communities claim and model both love and acceptance for humankind. Members of such communities commit time and energy to serving others. "Family," within the Caring Community concept, is extended to those who nurture and hold us accountable, regardless of race, gender, lineage, or religious affiliation. An important goal of Caring Communities is to provide a better quality of life, spiritual development, and critical thinking skills for all of its members, and any others desiring to affiliate. The Caring Community transmits its sacred and respected values to future generations by embracing cultural traditions, history, values, and legacies through storytelling. It preserves, respects, enables, and prods others to their higher selves. While the Caring Community has an expectation that each generation will build on the community's prior efforts and successes, it also fosters innovation and creativity. It has a humanistic value that is both spiritual and nonjudgmental.

Caring Communities can be identified through their acts of self-sufficiency, self-reliance, and nurturance of their youth and other vulnerable populations within the community. Caring Communities can actually be formed within villages, organizations, neighborhoods, churches, schools, non-for-profit organizations, corporations, and social groups, as long as they do not adapt the mission of these respective agencies. Members of these communities need to be free of prior claims on their time for the purpose of critical reflectivity, dreaming, and problematizing situations for a growth in awareness. Where there is a Caring Community, there is a place where individuals will find unconditional acceptance, values, and accountability. It is a place where lifelong learning occurs and serves as a foundation for moving beyond oneself in favor of a wider and more diverse extended family.

As indicated, Caring Communities are also genuinely concerned about the welfare of not only those they serve, but all of humanity. The concern has no boundaries; it is universal and boundless. Regardless of faith, each person within a Caring Community seeks to live out his or her faith life through a symbiotic relationship with others. The rule of thumb for the Caring Community is the universal Golden Rule: "Do unto others as you would have them to do unto You."

Caring Communities are composed of committed individuals who demonstrate enormous faith in humanity. As communities of faith,

Caring Communities strive to understand the plight of others and believe that fundamental to doing so is being able to also understand the culture, the history, and the traditions of those they serve or wish to serve, all the while searching for new meaning in their understanding of others and themselves. Acts of caring have always had the power to induce inner reflection. It is only by working through the tensions associated with our various differences that we are better able to appreciate our human diversity and grow in self awareness. Caring Communities use challenges as their curriculum for discussion, critique, and learning.

Because Caring Communities are "endowed groups" that are bound by ethics and humanistic values, they are markedly different from hate groups because they claim and model acceptance for all of humanity and differences of opinion. These communities set out to provide a better quality of life for all of its members, but they are also to be truth-tellers to themselves and other members.

The Role of Community in the Church

Although our churches speak of *saving* and *feeding* souls, many of us are not connecting with the unchurched. Moreover, some of us are not creating an inviting or nurturing atmosphere within our own congregations. Is it perhaps because we have not bothered to ensure that our congregations are nurturing? Caring Communities require attention as they are instrumental in forming *"vital congregations."* The process of forming these communities as effective enablers of ministry resembles learning organizations where the focus is on *process* as opposed to an end in itself. The Caring Community concept is at the heart of the Gospel. Disciples and other followers of Jesus Christ formed cohesive praying circles for the purpose of transformation through the Gospel. Today, these communities of care represent legacy bearers of the Gospel witnessing to the movement of the *Holy Spirit* working among and through us.

What laity, clergy, and the unchurched hold in common is a desire for personal acceptance and a place or movement where we find a strong connection to God and Jesus Christ through the shared word, worship, outreach ministries, and a loving and caring community. Yet while many churches have committee meetings, programs, and social events, few will formally announce that, for the purpose of discernment and visioning, they have formed a Caring Community. All churches may form these communities, but many view them as a waste of time or repetitive of the nurturing role already assigned to the church.

Once congregations determine the real value of Caring Communities, they are not restricted to calling them Caring Communities. What is far more important is that these groups not function in the same way as traditional and local church-structured organizations. The Caring Community emerges from a commitment that is mutually shared by its participants. And, while a Caring Community may be a subgroup of an entire congregation, no one person is ever in control of the process. The first stage in forming a Caring Community is bonding, which the facilitator-participant understands well. The most logical place to begin bonding within the church community is within already established Bible study groups and other Christian education programs. Once study group members have bonded and have completed their study process, the group may wish to continue meeting for purposes of nurturing and visioning. It is important to note that membership must always be voluntary, and although attendance is essential, there should also be an act of a covenantal agreement. Participation should be encouraged by the pastoral leader, who also participates freely as a coequal member of the nurturing community.

While Caring Communities may be intentionally formed within the body of the congregation, activities must move beyond superficial interactions. Attention must be given to providing members with a lens into their *hearts* and *souls* as well as the hearts and souls of others who share in the worship time with them. Caring Communities make sure there are opportunities for other members to become better acquainted with one another on a much deeper and more spiritual level. We must know our prayer partners' dreams, aspirations, spiritual challenges, and talents. Once we are able to identify our commonalities and our differences, we are far more likely to look beyond limitations and obstacles to much-needed mission and ministry.

Some churches devote time and energy to creating the culture for the development of Caring Communities as a part of their mission. These congregations provide all of the elements and gifts of Caring Communities. Their entire ministry has, as a goal, acts of nurturing, teaching, and reflecting. The Caring Community is a place that attracts visitors. When visitors enter the sanctuary, they are able to immediately "feel" the Caring Community, and while they might not be able to articulate why they feel different and better, they nonetheless verbalize a feeling of wellness, contentment, and expectancy. Just visit a vital church and experience the presence of a Caring Community. It is a powerful force similar to a magnet. You are attracted to the energy and power of these communities. You desire to affiliate with them because there is such a good feeling of joy and well-being radiating through the entire congregation.

On the other hand, if you enter a church sanctuary and feel uninvited, chances are you are experiencing a congregation that spreads the Gospel through its worship but is not living it through community. More than likely, members of this second type of congregation neither agree with nor are likely to be aligned with a compelling mission and vision. The reason is quite simple. It is because far less attention has been given to group bonding in those churches. Moreover, there has been no effort to reach congregants through the spiritual domain that is activated through our hearts. I have seen many of these congregations struggle as they follow all the blueprints for church vitality. Sadly, after striving to revitalize their congregations, they cannot understand why they do not attract new members.

In my consulting days, clergy and laity always seemed to know when something was not right, and they would rush quickly to find reasons to explain away problems and tensions. Oftentimes, the pastor and/or congregational leaders would be signaled out as their sources. This is unfortunate because, in doing so, members failed to look closely at their own collective external or public image. Furthermore, many members do not show a commitment to deeper levels of community building. Clearly, there is important work to do as congregations come to value the critical role they play in forming Caring Communities.

Transformational leadership must be facilitated by and within a community where hearts are touched through the care that is shown for the community's individual members. When transformation happens, people feel they have been impacted in profound ways. An inventory of these experiences has demonstrated that previously held assumptions can be transformed, values can be shifted, and people become far more capable of embracing change than ever before. Participants of these processes report becoming enlightened and most often transformed through acts of storytelling, testimonials, shared life experiences, and hands-on projects that touch hearts as well as the intellect (Preciphs 1989).

I have continuously rejoiced over experiencing the special care and nurturing I received in the African American neighborhood where I grew up in Dallas, Texas. The neighbors became my extended family, my educators, my accountability measure, and those who ensured my success in life. The elders gave their very best so the youth were grounded in positive values, motivation for education, and the love that continues to engulf my emotions. Without my amazing foundational experience of growing up in a Caring Community, I question whether I could have emerged as a responsible partner/collaborator and an effective leader. It is apparent that an investment in others is a form of disciple-making. Disciple-making goes hand-in-hand with church revitalization.

In our postmodern society, such communities are needed more than ever before in order to address depression, hopelessness, powerlessness, broken spirits, and an overwhelming sense of complexity within a fast-paced world. Too often, we assume that just because "we are the church," there is a ready-made fellowship capable of carrying out the church's mission. This assumption is as far from the truth as is the notion that fellowship hours, Christmas bazaars, and Easter pageants build community. Such activities have value, but it is a mistake to conclude that they translate into acts of care taking and nurturing.

Characteristics of a Caring Community include the following:

- Praying together and engaging in reflective practice
- Creating space and time for members to bond
- Building trust and mutual respect
- Granting permission for confronting assumptions and activities
- Accepting diversity and differences
- Taking risks through honesty and innovation
- Being accountable to the organizational mission
- Working through teams (balance of power)
- Sharing information
- Selecting outreach ministries that transform lives (givers and receivers)

- Keeping the focus on ethics and integrity
- Providing unity in purpose and direction
- Studying Scripture
- Empowering others through shared opportunities
- Challenging traditional ways of thinking and acting
- Visioning and discernment

While inviting open dialogue and discussion of members' and leaders' diverse ideas, it is important to understand that these discussion sessions are not intended to replicate or replace program planning, committee meetings, group therapy, or sessions related to conflict resolution. Instead, they are meant to focus on interpersonal dynamics and must facilitate a deeper appreciation and understanding of our prayer partners.

Sometimes sermons have real power in moving us from our logical thinking to our hearts. In this respect, the sacred worship hour can become the lens for activating the spiritual domain. Several years ago I heard a sermon in which a rural church pastor posed a question to his congregation that caused reflection and connected to my heart.

He inquired: "Why do you think so many of our youth are in prison, jail, or detention centers?"

Several members attempted to respond before the pastor answered his own question: "It is because we have stopped loving and caring for them."

This response captured my attention as I reflected on my own childhood experience. The elders in my neighborhood, along with members of my local church, cared more about our future and Christian maturation than they did about upward mobility or movement into a better life for themselves. Many of my elders had only an eighth grade education, but their desire was that all of the youth in our community would get an education and prove themselves worthy of the elders' investment of time and resources. Our elders were keen on building our characters and preparing us to succeed in life in ways they could only dream of. It was not easy growing up in the Jim Crow era, and even though life did not give much hope on many days, we were affirmed by these community elders, who were filled with love and hope for us. These were tough times, but we all knew that we were loved. It is their legacy that we are now charged with carrying out.

Sadly, I think that we have failed miserably in continuing the wonderful legacy we were left by the elders of our communities. I stand on this position because we have allowed the community care-taking role to be lost with the integration movement, attainment of increased levels of education, and the upward mobility spiral. The saying "It takes a village to raise a child" is the essence of the Caring Community. It is this philosophy, once fully embraced and celebrated by our community, that is now so starkly absent.

While the rural minister unknowingly called to my memory images of my elders' positive love, their unconditional acceptance, and their countless unselfish acts of giving, he was simultaneously a reminder of our unfulfilled promise and commitment to the youth of our day. Perhaps churches are struggling to maintain their membership and vitality because, in spite of our recitation of Gospel legacies, we struggle daily with the distractions of the world. In spite of what we say, we seem to be both in the world and of the world. We invite people to affiliate with us but seem to have tremendous difficulty nurturing them holistically.

Within our postmodern society, we are all challenged by complexities, fast-paced lifestyles, and an explosion of information that bombards us at every turn. The reality is that we no longer prioritize "community" as the primary value we once did. We are so very busy reacting to our world that we are not being proactive in helping to reshape it. To transform our individual churches into Caring Communities, we must view community caretaking as the foundation of mission and ministry. Caretaking communities are repositories of hope and bridges and are capable of facilitating vision and other transformation and conversion experiences.

Bible studies are perhaps the most powerful bonding acts where churches and Caring Communities can participate because these study sessions can effectively link Scripture to postmodern realities. Bible studies can also provide opportunities for smaller groups of individuals to be able to interact with each other through sharing their own life stories, struggles, and journeys, thereby enabling the affective domain to enter. Many individuals in dissimilar groups have found far stronger friendships and many more commonalities through activities that revolve around building fellowship and Caring Communities.

One of the greatest challenges to churches is the acceptance of people who are different in appearance, habits, language, and culture. However, unless we are able to see the value in such diversity, our mission outreach programs will certainly be hampered even before they are implemented. As we move beyond superficial acts of community building and bonding to a place where we know and trust the members of the community better, we will become much more equipped to address and even eliminate conflicts.

In the modern era, communities did not have a choice about whether or not they needed to bond, collaborate, and work in harmony. Disenfranchised people understood that it was only through a Caring Community that they could remain whole and intact. For example, during the 1920s–1950s our founder, Dr. Mary McLeod Bethune, held town hall meetings designed to empower the community. Because they, too, were in search of empowerment, even white women attended Dr. Bethune's town hall meetings during the Jim Crow era. It seemed a natural thing for them to do because, in Bethune, they saw a woman whose message and conduct transcended race, gender, and class.

Dr. Bethune held the philosophy that the problems any community faced could and should be addressed and solved by that very same community. Of course, this was prior to the government's support of its underserved populations. Dr. Bethune taught people how to work together as a Caring Community in order to lift one another up. She provided food for residents of the community as well as her students by plowing the land so crops could be grown and by raising cattle and chickens. She also addressed problems facing the community's young people as well as voter registration for women and people from African descent. Because she built such powerful relationships among community stakeholders, one day she was tipped off by a white Episcopal priest that the Klan was planning to pay her campus a visit because of their outrage over the increased voter registration of African Americans.

As promise keepers of the Gospel, we learn much more about ourselves when we are in a trusting community. Mental health workers use group therapy and place clients into communities as an effective intervention. Many organizations employ cross-functional teams that mimic Caring Communities in order to bring about more productive outcomes. Vital congregations employ Caring Communities to lead people to Christ and Christ's church.

Effective organizations ensure a healthy balance between visionary (transformative leaders) and managerial (transactional managers) leadership. An imbalance between these two leadership styles places an organization at risk for vulnerabilities in both sound management and/ or innovation. Both leadership styles are dependent on expertise that stems from a variety of traits, qualities, and characteristics. The question of whether a leader should possess a balance of transformative and transactional leadership styles is continuously asked, and the answer is predicated on the belief that each leader will, in fact, express a dominant leadership style. This dominant style will naturally emerge. Interestingly, in many instances, transactional and transformative leaders may, in fact, be oblivious to what their leadership style is.

Within Caring Communities, we need participation by both leadership styles to enlarge our thinking and to explore the paradigms held within diverse leadership styles.

Transformation Can Be Both Painful and Rewarding

My life has always been characterized by a passion for looking beyond myself for ways in which I could be of service to others. Because I had been raised in Caring Communities and knew what they looked like and how they made you feel, I was also very keenly aware of the stark absence of such communities. My life and the work I saw for myself as a servant leader was not unlike Naomi's life inasmuch as she, too, was committed to serving Ruth even though their formal relationship had been severed because of the death of her husband. I embraced the spirit of service when I was hired to serve a national women's advocacy agency as part of a three-person coequal CEO. Our mandate revolved around such issues as: (1) upward mobility in career paths; (2) the use of inclusive language; (3) the placement of women into top leadership positions; and (4) equity in compensation.

My passion for serving others only intensified when I traveled to Kenya and observed women who barely had enough food to feed their families. I was in awe as I learned that they were walking three miles or more to attend our United Nations conference. These women were like Naomi, who gleaned after the reapers. Naomi thought nothing of walking or running after the reaper to gather much needed sustenance, and neither did my Kenyan sisters. They willingly walked miles because, for them, our conferences provided a special kind of sustenance. They were hungry for spiritual food and were determined to put themselves in the place where they could receive it.

While in Kenya, I became greatly concerned when I became aware of the personal trials of our driver, a man who always wore a smile on his face. Soon I learned that this same man, a husband and father, had no running water, no money to buy medicine, and that he and his wife had recently lost one of their young children to malaria.

It was at that moment that I began to question my agency's mission. The critique and reflection was facilitated by my participation in a community of faith-based individuals who listened to my inquiries about assumptions. Being brought face-to-face with the "life and death" issues that our driver's wife and millions of women around the world were constantly assailed by somehow relegated my agency's issues to a position of relative unimportance in the larger scheme of things. Career upward mobility and language inclusiveness became myopic and anemic when viewed with lenses that included not having money to purchase live-giving medicine and the death of a child who had just begun life's journey.

My encounter with the specifics of our driver's life affected me in far more fundamental ways than, at that time, I realized. Today, I understand with a growing awareness and sensitivity just how easy it is to move through powerful experiences of transformative leadership and yet be unable to recognize the impact of such experience—to be changed without understanding how or to what extent. This is precisely what happened to me those many years ago. Without being consciously aware, my life had been transformed by and through these experiences in ways that would forever motivate me to be much more compassionate and to be a very different kind of leader. As I reflect on this experience, I remember having a total sense of discomfort. I did not feel safe to share my feelings with the women's advocacy agency where I served. I did not want my new level of consciousness to take away from their needs, but I had to respect the new level of understanding that had emerged from a significant emotional experience. I was confused and also had a feeling of being a traitor because I could no longer prioritize their goals that included upward mobility and inclusive language. Many of our mission statements and goals are concerned with looking inward rather than outward. *My women's advocacy agency had not realized that in an attempt to empower American women, they had overlooked the plight of all women.*

I was very fortunate to find another safe and nurturing community, beyond my immediate reference group, that would sit with me and take a journey into the transformative world of dialogue, critique and reflection. Little did I know at the time the importance of having a Caring Community to help facilitate my personal and dramatic transformation. It was the Caring Community that enabled me to challenge the status quo within my women's advocacy agency that ironically had set forth a mission to democratize systems and people, but had failed to see its own shortcomings.

I became aware that it is possible to have multiple Caring Communities with differing mandates. However, each Caring Community that one identifies with should be capable of facilitating internal reflection on reality. For instance, the national women's agency continued to provide important impetus and learning that was extremely helpful in shifting my belief system and perspectives in other areas, even though many of their priorities were no longer important as a consequence of my experience in Africa.

The powerful Kenyan experience resonated deeply within, leaving me with the persistent and uncomfortable feeling that I had forgotten to do something really important but just could not quite recall what it was. Many of us often have this uneasy feeling, which is both distracting and unsettling! I have learned that when I am unsettled, it is the very time to engage a Caring Community to test and probe for insights and possible new awareness. It is true that any aspects of the transformation process remain a mystery; however, through critical reflection within community, people become much more predisposed to both understand and welcome change. True change is first facilitated through a significant emotional experience, which is precisely what led to my transformation.

Over the course of several months, the differences between the stark realities faced by my Kenyan brothers and sisters and those of their Western counterparts bombarded me, and I found myself becoming more and more resentful of American women whose cultural sensitivity was severely lacking. This lack of sensitivity to global issues resulted in my becoming, in the words of African novelist Chinua Achebe, "no longer at ease." These same women were also insensitive to minority individuals, whose lack of power and privilege was also readily apparent in the lives of the men and women I met and interacted with in Kenya. I came to the rather sad but unavoidable conclusion that the women who were driving the processes at my agency and with whom I spent countless waking hours took their privilege and their power for granted.

Like the Sankofa bird, I looked back over my experiences in Kenya even as I continued to move forward. There was no question that I had been deeply affected by the time I spent with my Kenyan brothers and sisters; however, the impact of these experiences had yet to manifest itself in overt ways following my return to the United States. That would soon change. In response to the transformation, I tendered my resignation with the agency seven years after first joining its staff and four years after my return from Kenya.

No, I have not always understood the power of transformative thinking nor of leading as a transformative leader. But I have come to appreciate the power of both, and I dearly wish that I had been introduced to and therefore knew to employ these important processes during my early weeks and months as a young employee at my women's advocacy agency. If the leadership of churches, schools, and businesses is to truly change their respective environments to places where diversity is genuinely accepted, the contributions of members valued, and traditional ways of thinking and responding rejected, transformative learning and, ultimately, evolution into a transformative leader are imperative.

While I became disappointed with my women's advocacy agency, I must again clarify that the failure of a Caring Community, like this agency, on one issue or concern does not mean that the same community is incapable of fostering critique and growth on other topics that produce necessary transformation. The story below about Jim makes this case.

From the late '60s to '70s, The United Methodist Church in the United States created two national advocacy agencies that enabled the denomination to break out of its traditional patterns of thinking and acting toward people of color and women. I had the privilege of serving as an administrator investigator for inclusiveness in a mainline denomination. Seven of those years were spent working for the General Commission on the Status and Role of Women, a national women's advocacy agency. The Commission was composed of forty-five members from the United States. A majority of the Commission's members were completing a second term of service and had a history with the organization.

During my seven years with the Commission, we welcomed a newly appointed member who was to serve a four-year term in the quadrennium. This new member of the Commission was an attorney from Alaska and was assigned to my policy unit, a unit that addressed education for social change and handled investigations into alleged cases of gender discrimination. Keep in mind that during this time, the denomination was in the midst of a cultural shift in ideology, which would have the effect of ensuring the acceptance of women into leadership positions at all levels (i.e., ordained, ministry, administrative roles, and program oversight, etc.). As a directive from the highest legislative body within that denomination, our charge was to bring about systemic change on behalf of women. Yet, for many, change was exceedingly difficult. The lawyer from Alaska, whom I will simply refer to as Jim, was extraordinarily hostile in his behavior toward the work of our Commission. He was also demeaning of female leadership. He was also quite obnoxious and elitist in his approach and manner.

Throughout the Commission's first meeting with Jim, he presented himself as "the" expert on each topic introduced for discussion. He was confrontational toward our process and became the self-appointed attorney-in-residence. Within two days of his tenure, Jim had managed to insult every female administrator, every female commissioner, and even most of the male commissioners. His actions made almost everyone feel inferior, insulted, and demeaned. I was shocked and troubled, especially since Jim's annual conference judicatory had just elected him to membership in our agency. I was even more concerned because Jim had been specifically assigned to my work unit for the next four years. As difficult as it was to fathom, Jim had actually been charged with supporting the mission of democratizing the denomination by moving to empower women at all levels and judicatories. To say that our unit's membership was demoralized is an understatement.

Jim had done real damage to the unit's morale, confidence, and sense of purpose, and after assessing the damage, the unit's members felt compelled to stop its meeting in order to confront him. Over the next few minutes, Jim was given feedback that was candid and bold. There was little else we could do if we were to reclaim the dignity and self-respect that Jim had so effectively robbed us of in the short span of a few hours.

As I reflect on Jim's actions, I am reminded of Dennis Kimbro's "pumpkin story." It is the story of a farmer who, while working in his field one day, came across a one-gallon jug. With nothing better to do, and in an experimental mindset, the farmer took a very small pumpkin and thrust it into the opening of the jug. He left the one-gallon jug in his field with no plans or inclination to do anything else with it. Almost a full year passed and the farmer returned to the field to a surprising find. Rather than grow to the point of breaking out of the gallon jug, the pumpkin had grown to the exact size and shape of the container and then appeared to have stopped growing. The restrictions that the gallon jug had imposed on the pumpkin effectively prevented the pumpkin from doing anything more or different than it had done (1992). The pumpkin was confined and restricted to the gallon jug just as people in church bodies, colleges and universities, and workplace environments are often confined and restricted by the assumptions they hold, as well as self-imposed parameters and limitations.

It is very likely that Jim responded in the only way he knew. Jim's "gallon jug" was his socialization process, his prejudices, his biases, and the firmly held assumptions he brought with him. Based on these unfortunate realities, Jim took the only "shape" that he could.

We felt challenged, just as Paul felt when he encountered Peter's treatment toward the Gentiles when the Jews appeared on the scene in Antioch. Peter's actions were public, and like Paul, we needed to make our response to Jim's assault on us public. His opposition to our goals had been seen, heard, and felt within a public forum. Jim had not minced words, and neither could we. Pollock puts it this way, "Paul could not oppose Peter privately. The damage was public; the opposition must be public if the faith were to be secured for all men everywhere" (Pollock 1972).

Although I left my employment with the Commission several months later to assume another position with another national agency, I was invited back a year later for a special tribute. Jim spoke; I listened and, frankly, was amazed. Contrary to my expectations, I found him to be a most sensitive and caring individual on issues that were specific to women. Moreover, Jim showed this same care and sensitivity to broader diversity issues and concerns. He shared with the members of the audience the consensus decision-making process and personally demonstrated his respect for other commissioners. There was no doubt in my mind that Jim was a transformed individual. It is possible that somewhere between the time I left the organization and my return for the tribute, Jim had participated in certain transformative learning experiences and a variety of other educational programs that resulted in his transformation. But at that time, I wondered what actually produced this change in Jim. As an educator, I soon realized that I was faced with a rare opportunity. If I could discover and then study the process of Jim's transformation, I would be able to unearth how deeply held belief systems and values are shifted!

I was pleased to see that the agency had redeemed itself as a transforming force for change that brought value to all of humanity. It was further reassuring to know that although a valued organization falls short of our expectations, it can still be vital in many other ways.

Over the next two years, I was blessed with the opportunity to study the process of transformation, the end of which netted me some remarkable findings. Simply put, individuals change their belief systems and values *only* as the result of the process of accessing the "affective domain of learning." Clearly, this was a major breakthrough to a critical paradigm shift, a shift that held as the desirable product change that was lasting rather than ephemeral, a shift that moved beyond mandated and obligatory behavioral change to a change in core beliefs and values. It is precisely through the process of accessing the affective domain of learning that *long-held assumptions are framed for a re-evaluation and re-ordering of mental models and paradigms* observable by both organizations and those that lead them (Mezirow 1990).

My research findings led me to substitute the theological term "spiritual domain" in place of the more academic term "affective domain." This was because I now viewed the process of change as an opening into a spiritual dimension of learning where emotions and feelings are accessed and engaged, and where people can then move forward to reexamine their beliefs, perceptions, and attitudes about a great many topics, issues, situations, circumstances, events, people, races, communities, and nations.

In particular, leaders of churches, schools, and businesses can be looked to for innovation, change, and yes, leadership. It is extremely important to point out that accessing the affective domain does not automatically result in change. When we access the spiritual domain, we are capable of actually creating the atmosphere that is a precursor or prerequisite for a deeper level of reflection to occur, which may well lead to change.

You have been reading a challenge—a righteous challenge, if you will. My challenge is to clergypeople, business leaders, nonprofit executives, and student leaders. I am asking you to commit yourself to the process that resulted in my becoming a transformational thinker and a transformative leader, something the world is in dire need of. The challenge is for the church and other organizations to form and sustain communities that will dare to engage in critique and exploration in order to probe new insights, ideas, and visions for the future.

Finally, the importance of this story is the emergence of a new understanding of how and why we move from discomfort caused by a disjunction between our logical side and our emotions to an examination of our traditional beliefs. In and of itself, discomfort is not negative; it is a sign that we are in need of a safe community in which to explore our feelings. Discomfort is often the beginning of a conflict between the "head" and the "heart," and if facilitated through community dialogue, can lead to greater critique and reflection. Once the heart is touched, the logical reasoning mechanism takes a back seat. This is then the time for an awakening of the spiritual domain to much-needed engagement in the transformative processes.

My journey toward an understanding of transformative leadership had not occurred in my earlier career when I tried without success to shift perspectives and behaviors on issues of diversity. I have since learned that while shifts in behavior may only be temporary, changes in our perspectives are lasting and enable us to overcome the "isms" that have divided nations and our world.

The point of the Kenyan story is that one does not have to be a participant in a Caring Community at the time a significant emotional experience or inner conflict takes place. Previous involvement with a Caring Community allows us to draw from our past, as we utilize the process of critical reflection needed for self-critique. The case of the Kenyan story demonstrates this point as I automatically reverted back to previous communities of care for guidance as soon as I was confronted with new knowledge about the hunger and health crisis impacting the women and children of Kenya. This is another reason Caring Communities are so very different than just any other group. Not only do Caring Communities place primary focus on humanistic goals, but they also teach us how to pause, reflect, and seek wisdom for our inner struggles.

Chapter II

Transformative Leadership: Activating The Spiritual Domain

Like my experience at my alma mater, many of us over the age of fifty have participated in consciousness-raising groups or exercises designed to address human oppression and to empower those who experienced it while working with the majority culture in the United States. Consciousness-raising events of that time period often involved homogeneous groups of people who shared common visions and values. Skill workshops were unsuccessful as we had focused our intervention on shifting attitudes and behavior. Too often, the focus of our training events was on effecting change that just did not take root. As I reflect, most of those experiences were intellectual pursuits that attempted to help people accept differences and diversity based on logic and reasoning. Because I had not yet been exposed to transformative leadership, I now understand that what was unclear at the time was that any organizational change using skill-based learning would have resulted only in limited and short-lived modifications of behavior.

What we failed to do was to place focus on individual transformation in beliefs as opposed to behavioral changes. Such is the case with Affirmative Action, which was forced behavioral change that did not sustain systemic nor individual transformation toward the acceptance of people who are different in cultural heritage, tradition, and history. Another problem with incorporating Affirmative Action in organizations was that the rationale was based on logical, rational thinking processes without regard for the need to get people emotionally connected with those who were different. If Affirmative Action had included making an emotional connection between diverse populations of people, the avenue of inclusiveness would have been embraced and welcomed, and the long-term effects of the goals for systemic change would be owned and lasting. Because the educational process of transformation can employ the spiritual domain of learning, it is capable of shifting both behavior and values. The spiritual domain of learning, if activated, is a powerful force for transition of individuals and then their organizations. Transformative leadership is an ongoing process of learning that can also engage the spiritual domain and is the foundation of innovation, visioning, and creativity impacting self and others. Real change within our value system is driven by *significant emotional experiences* that move our logic aside in order for the heart to speak to our soul. For the church and other religious communities, we understand that God speaks to us through our hearts.

This form of leadership is a continuous learning process whereby leaders and their stakeholders are liberated from traditional barriers of thinking that impede vision, creativity, and respect for humanity. Individual participation in a Caring Community provides an effective lens into one's values and beliefs through critical reflection (Preciphs 1989).

Formerly, I had assumed that the critique of assumptions and reflection within Caring Communities was all that was needed to prod and question traditional beliefs. However, I now have come to understand that this is only one aspect of transformative leadership. Another aspect of transformative leadership is touching the heart to activate the spiritual domain.

The following story describes how my
"heart" challenged my behavior.

Almost fifty summers ago, I heard a loud knock at our front door. I was home alone, and knowing not to open the door, I peered from behind the curtain to observe a white man standing at the locked screened door. I had been cautioned and specifically instructed never to open the door to strangers otherwise I might be harmed. Without consciously willing it, memories associated with watching Nana pay burial fees all those years flooded my spirit and, without thinking, I snapped at the stranger in a hostile and anything but Christian tone.

Now, I just wanted to know what this stranger wanted from us. I can still picture the screened-in porch where the lock was set and where

I stood as I queried the stranger. I felt justified in questioning him about why he was coming to my neighborhood and why he was taking advantage of poor people. It turned out that he was selling pencils and other small items. His hope was that we would purchase something from him. Unfortunately for this particular stranger, standing on the other side of our screened-in and locked porch, my past anger and resentment for white salesmen surged, and he became its unsuspecting victim. His appearance at our front door served as the detonator for the time bomb of ill feelings and anger connected to many similar knocks of yesteryear. In my mind's eye, I could see my grandmother paying her policy bill all over again. My subsequent comments to the stranger were harsh and cruel—two things that I am not. In response, the stranger looked into my face and, with sadness, stated simply, "I am just hungry and trying to make a living."

At that very moment, hurt and shame flooded through me. My words and actions were not me at all. Even though my unkind words were aimed at the stranger, I felt that I was responsible for a self-inflicted wound to my own spirit because I was usually loving and kind toward everyone. I couldn't have been more than nine or ten years old. My mean-spirited comments had overshadowed my higher self and the respect it had always been important for me to give others—regardless of who they were. I was guilty of allowing conclusions, arrived at through my past experiences, to be transferred to perhaps an innocent person. I stood there feeling ashamed and convicted by my deeds as countless thoughts ran through my mind. As I reflected on that brief exchange, I concluded that the stranger had, in fact, seemed sincere. A solitary question pounded my head: "What if he really is hungry?"

My heart sank lower and lower as I watched the stranger back away from our front door and walk down the walkway and then the sidewalk in front on the houses in our block. I knew that I had wounded this person who might well have been even needier than my own family, whose members were also out trying to make a living. I knew that as a Christian I had failed.

At that moment, I turned and quickly went into our kitchen to make the white pencil salesman a ham sandwich from food left over from our Sunday meal. I quickly wrapped the sandwich in wax paper and placed it in a brown paper bag. I ran as fast as I could out of the screened porch area, trying desperately to catch up with the stranger, who had decided against stopping at the next set of houses on my block.

I did catch up with the stranger and, once standing in front of him, said, "Sir, I have something for you." My biting comments no doubt still held their sting, and I can't begin to imagine what he must have thought of me as I stood there offering him something to eat. He just looked dejected and very tired. It is still difficult for me to describe how I felt when he put his hand out to take the bag from me. I was glad but still so ashamed of my earlier behavior that I quickly turned and left him to hold on to whatever dignity he still had. I couldn't help but look back as I ran toward to my house. And what I saw was a man who was hungry. I saw a man unwrapping and then taking a bite out of a sandwich as though it might well be the only thing he would have to eat that day. I saw a man who God had sent to our front door that we might show ourselves members of his family by feeding "the least of these." I saw a man who only needed someone to care—an act made possible only when he and others like him can encounter the Caring Community.

The Kingdom of God was never intended to be static. Instead, it is a dynamic and transformative life-changing force that moves with and among all of humanity, including those strangers in our midst! If we claim God as our eternal king, our ministry must be consumed with innovative and creative acts to spread God's Kingdom here on earth. These acts should not be focused only within the church house, but in every walk of life, including on the other side of my front door. The sad truth is that we commit very little effort to reaching the strangers on our streets in order to offer them the Gospel of Jesus Christ. Our faith-based efforts must be concerned with programs that "feed" the stranger spiritually as well as physically. We must not be found waiting for them to show up at our door; instead, we must become serious about leaving behind the familiarity and perceived safety of the four walls of our respective churches.

Too many churches only offer hospitality to those who show up for worship on Sunday mornings. How many more would enter the church door on Sunday if we were found working during the week in the fields as the shepherds we have been commissioned by God to be? Central to the New Testament is Jesus' proclamation and announcement of the "Kingdom of God." This phrase is discussed thirty-two times in the Book of Matthew and eighty times throughout the Gospel. What does the Kingdom of God really mean to us in our faith walk as Christians and clergypeople?

I was forever transformed by a stranger fifty years ago. It was a transformation that helped me bear witness to the gifts of a Caring Community. I know that I will never again transfer my problems onto others as I had initially done with that stranger. I will always be thankful that he accepted my gift of the sandwich because, in the eyes of a nine year old, it meant I had been forgiven. Even though I was, at that time, unable to articulate the transformation that had occurred in my life, I now understood that true service to humanity is akin to becoming a shepherd for spreading the Gospel of Jesus Christ.

My encounter with the stranger of my youth touched my heart in ways that my Sunday school classes could not have accomplished. This was a transformative experience and a movement of the Holy Spirit in my life toward the ideals and action of a Caring Community. This experience awakened my soul toward building God's Kingdom and served as an epiphany of what the Gospel is really about.

The words in the Scripture recorded in Matthew 25:35–36 had come alive. "For when I was hungry and you gave me food, I was thirsty and you gave me something to drink, I was a stranger and you welcomed me, I was naked and you gave me clothing, I was sick and you took care of me, I was in prison and you visited me." I suddenly understood why Nana embraced the stranger but kept her real trust in God. When Nana died at age ninety-two, no burial policies were found. But Nana trusted God and had a beautiful church service and the finest funeral and burial that I have ever experienced.

The fact that I ran after the stranger was directly related to the values that had been ingrained in me as a member of the endowed Caring Community that raised me and the young people I was fortunate to grow up alongside. Flying out of my front door, carrying a sandwich I had made from meat left from our Sunday meal was an exercise in the accountability I felt as a product of a Caring Community. The ethics of the Caring Community where I was raised made it impossible for me to respond in any other way. Because I was the product of a community of people that loved one another and embraced one another, my initial perspective about the stranger was transformed. This illustration demonstrates another facet of one's participation in a

Caring Community. We do not always need to be seated and reflecting, in person, with a Caring Community in order to extract the values that are needed to facilitate internal critique and reflection. Once our hearts have been touched, we easily reflect back to those sacred values that we are gifted with from our Caring Communities.

Like my story of the stranger, today's congregations, as well as people outside of the church, seemed to have been socialized not to care about their neighbors, let alone the strangers in their midst. Unlike the Good Samaritan, we pass homeless people as well as young people on the streets. We can see they are in trouble, and yet we look the other way and tell ourselves that these people are none of our business.

Because of the values I extracted from my Caring Community, I was open to truly experiencing transformation with the stranger. We are also able to seek insights from multiple communities that dare to challenge our thinking or traditions. Transformative leadership is truly continuous, contagious, and ongoing.

The Heart—A Place Where God Speaks to Us

A major challenge for all organizations is their inability to bridge the gulf between recognizing that change is needed and accepting the changes in valued and subsequent behavior that are, in fact, called for by the recognition of the need to make changes. Many of us grasp for new models for dying congregations but refuse to change our behavior or thinking to make shifts in our ministries. As we now understand, the process of transformation is derived from a spiritual dimension that is made manifest from instruction from the Holy Spirit as God moves among and through us. Real change—change that is lasting—is only possible through the agency of the Holy Spirit where our hearts are touched. God is concerned about the matters of the heart, and God alone understands the human heart. The fact that the word "heart" is mentioned in the Bible some 825 times is no coincidence. Only the words "Lord" and "God" are mentioned more. "Jesus," "faith," "wisdom," "praise" and several other key words are mentioned in Scripture far fewer times. The following offers just a few examples of the abundant use of the word "heart" in Scripture.

The Human Heart—
The Lens into the Spiritual Domain

Matt. 22:37—"Love the Lord thy God with all thy Heart."
Matt. 5:8—"... Pure in heart."
Matt. 12:34—"... abundance of the heart."
Matt. 6:21—"... there will your heart be also."
Luke 2:51—"... all things in her heart."
Luke 6:45—"... treasure of his heart."
Luke 16:15—"God knoweth your heart."
John 14:1—"Let not your heart be troubled ..."
John 16:22—"... your heart shall rejoice. "
Acts 4:32—"... of one heart."
Rom. 8:27—"... searcheth the hearts."
Eph. 3:17—"... Christ dwelling in your heart ..."
1 Cor. 2:9—"... Heart of man ..."
1 Pet. 1:22—"... a pure heart."

According to Scripture, only God understands our hearts. It follows then that when we enter the spiritual domain of learning (that place where our feelings, emotions, and passions reside, deep inside each human heart) we end up being drawn closer to God and closer to God's will for our lives. It is through this communion with God that we can experience transformation and lasting change.

It is God's desire that each of us be transformed (changed) just as Saul was changed. John Pollock writes of Saul's transformation into Paul, saying, "His entire body was in mutation. He was being turned inside out as he let Jesus light the recesses of his soul" (Pollock). It is clear that, at its highest point, accessing the spiritual domain and communion with the Holy Spirit are one. The proof of this contact is readily evident in the spiritually rich chills, tears, sobs, and the tender warmth that suddenly encases the body each time fellowship with the Holy Spirit takes place. I am convinced that entering the spiritual domain means to come into fellowship with the Holy Spirit. I am equally certain that it is only through communion with the Holy Spirit, made possible through accessing the affective domain of learning, that institutions and organizations will achieve the degree and the type of transformation requisite for addressing the stagnation or death of churches, businesses, and institutions of higher learning.

Through the spiritual dimension of leadership we receive instruction from the Holy Spirit as God moves among and through us. Real change—change that is lasting—is only possible through the agency of the Holy Spirit. Through the spiritual domain (heart) we are mandated by God for acts of kingdom building. God is concerned about the matters of the heart and God alone understands the human heart.

Activating the Spiritual Domain

I've spoken a lot about the spiritual domain and want to share some of the lenses into the doorway of the spiritual domain. The significance of mission/outreach ministry is that it serves as an important lens into the spiritual domain of transformative leadership. Until congregations and other organizational leaders move into experiences where they reach and have direct contact with those on the highways and byways, they remain in a logical, left-brain thinking mode. Limited transformation and visioning occurs in this manner because programs and events are traditionally constructed and delivered. Many churches speak of reaching the unchurched but do not go directly to these people to spiritually and physically feed them, as in the case of the homeless. Yet this kind of mission outreach gives a lens for others who are in need.

According to recent statistics released by the Covenant House of Fort Lauderdale, a charitable organization that supports homeless youth, 40 percent of the homeless people in America are under the age of eighteen, and those who are moving out of foster care or juvenile justice because of having reached majority age will become homeless within their first six months of release because there is no genuinely Caring Community to claim them as its own (Covenant House 2008). In John 12:32, Jesus said, "If I be lifted up from the earth, I will draw all [people] unto me." If we were being tested, and in truth, we are, churches and the community as a whole would fail miserably.

We make numerous excuses as to why we just walk right past those we know need our help, our support, and our encouragement. We tell ourselves that we don't want to be exploited, physically harmed, or have our kindness taken for weakness. Unlike Nana, we do not trust God to take care of us as we show kindness and hospitality to the strangers we encounter. The real loss is our own because in denying them, we deny ourselves the opportunity for God to do a mighty work with and through us. My own experience with the stranger who knocked on our door hungry and trying to sell pencils to earn money for food happened over fifty years ago. And, yet, this image lives with me daily. Its power to transform has continued to feed my spirit.

God has a process for change that confronts our assumptions, beliefs, and actions through the heart. Our transformation from shared life experiences and significant emotional experiences is central to the recognition that God is always calling us to newness by enlarging our awareness of self and others. Change is necessary for kingdom building. Transformation pulls at us; it stirs our souls, minds, and hearts to new understandings about salvation and God's love for us. Transformation calls forth newness, thus emancipating us from our past. Transformation reminds us that we are instruments of God rather than systems and organizations. We are servants to God and God's will for the world.

Transformation that is driven by the spiritual domain is about the *Holy Spirit* at work in us. Through community in dialogue, we are aided in reflecting on the entrenchment of beliefs and thought processes that, in actuality, are barriers to the *Holy Spirit*. Transformative leadership has the capacity to remove barriers, allowing God to communicate with us through insights, feelings, and actions. Transformative leadership has the capacity to free us from such worldly matters as control, the desire for power to dominate others, and competition for self gain. Transformative and conversion experiences are enabling forces that unravel worldly aspirations so that an ongoing relationship with God and Jesus Christ can be established. In this process, we are allowed to release the old baggage that inhibits spiritual growth. Transformative learning helps us bring to the surface both hidden and known assumptions in finding new pathways, roadmaps, and radical changes in our direction for ourselves, our congregations, and outreach ministries. Transformational leadership is how God speaks to us once we have removed barriers and mental blocks caused by traditional thinking and reasoning that impede mission, ministry, and our own spiritual growth and development. This form of leadership works at stripping away worn-out assumptions and worldly needs just long enough for change to occur toward kingdom building.

For the academic community, service learning and volunteerism is a critical lens for activating the spiritual domain of learning. Service learning is a curriculum-based activity in which volunteerism becomes the vehicle for learning and serving. Moreover, service learning and mission outreach work are akin and allow faith-based groups to engage in transformative learning. For church organizations, mission outreach work is the lens. Movement away from homogeneous groups to viewing how others live and work constitutes a learning praxis for the faith community. Moreover, living among those who are without the luxuries of our standard forms of living, or experiencing worship forms of truly oppressed people, is an invaluable way to take a journey into self and a critique of one's values.

Once the foundation is solidly placed, transformation of one's spirit, transition in beliefs and values, and visioning can become a reality. It is clear, the process of transformation in values and beliefs is facilitated by a significant emotional experience wherein the groundwork has already been laid within a nurturing community (Preciphs 1989).

The Process of Transformation

Consider the transformative process to be a continuous learning endeavor that remains with us throughout life. Does this mean that we are all perpetual learners? The answer lies with the Gospel, where Jesus Christ shared stories with both the unsaved and his disciples. Although there were different levels of awareness and depth, Christ chose to continuously challenge the thinking of all constituents, even though the disciples had a deeper level of the Gospel. Learning is never an end itself, nor are transformative leadership processes. Transformative leadership is dependent on effective facilitators who embrace the philosophy and definition of this movement of the heart and mind. Whether the facilitator-leaders are within Caring Communities or organizations that derive benefit from such entities, these individuals must be trained and capable of leading without judging and controlling the outcome of discussion, critique, or reflections. Their major role is leading individuals and groups on a journey of self and organizational discovery.

The transformative process begins with the role of facilitator-leader, who lays the foundation for building a Caring Community … a community where ideas are freely shared; where participants learn about one another as they form a culture of respect; where assumptions are critiqued without judgment or fear; and where traditional thinking is constantly evaluated. Through individual and group reflection, discernment and visioning what is new becomes possible. These facilitator-leaders may be CEOs, pastors, consultants, or individual followers who are capable of leading this learning process. However, each person has equal power, and positions of authority must not inhibit this process.

This transformative process is described in adult education literature, within the theory of emancipatory learning, as a process that creates conditions that make room for revisiting our habitual ways of thinking and reviewing perspectives. According to adult education theorist Jack Mezirow, perspective transformation is an emancipatory process of:

> *Becoming critically aware of why and how the structure of psycho-cultural assumptions have come to constrain the way we see ourselves and our relationships, reconstituting the structure to permit a more inclusive and discriminating integration of experience and acting upon these understandings.*

Mezirow describes changes in beliefs as "perspective transformation" because the process is internal to the adult learner. My thesis combines with this understanding but makes known the importance of the Caring Community's role in fostering the reflective practice of leaders and their followers.

As shown in **Figure 2**, the transformational praxis describes the symbiotic relationship between community care-taking and conditions conducive to transformation. It also demonstrates the important role of a facilitator of this learning process.

FIGURE 2

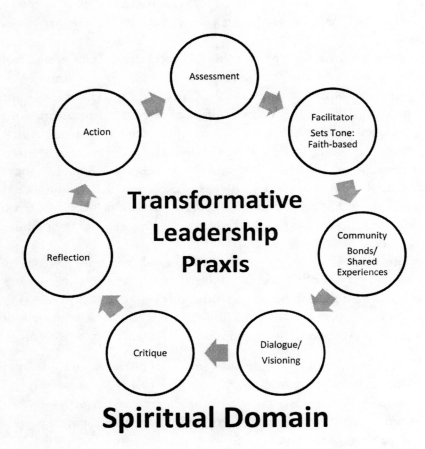

To activate the affective (spiritual) domain, facilitators often utilize storytelling, shared life experiences, testimonials, service learning, and outreach mission projects to trigger significant emotional experiences that open the doorway to the heart. Within our Christian context, we often describe this stage as discernment of God's movement with and through us. Many of my research study participants described the transformative process as the Holy Spirit at work as they framed new realities and saw a new vision. The transformative process is one in which individuals and groups move to new and innovative levels.

The result of reaching these new levels is new insights that position individuals for possible acts of behavioral or value transition. This process works differently for each participant. Some people experience dramatic transition in thinking, while others continue to reflect and discern. Some remain completely unchanged. The process of transformative leadership does not assume an outcome. Rather, the process is principally and primarily concerned with an "opening of a learning space" for critical reflection and for the Holy Spirit to work.

From time to time, we are all guilty of having myopic vision. It is only through process of transformative learning that we receive corrective lenses for each act of decision-making, discernment, and embracing needed desired change. Change for the sake of change should **never** be the goal of transformative leadership. Conversely, organic organizations must intentionally and periodically review, as well as critique, traditional programs, action goals, and directions for effective organizations.

Many organizations fear change, as it threatens the status quo and its individual stakeholders. Resistance to change is commonplace for all organizations. When we see change, we take offense and target the leader. This fear of change is often related to leaders not adequately being prepared for the process of change that can occur as a result of the spiritual domain. Leaders often gain new insights and vision resulting from some significant emotional experience that has been a part of some Caring Community. The struggle to change can be scary for followers and leaders alike because it involves greater risk-taking if the organization has failed to create and nurture Caring Communities that drive the change.

The quote "Silence cannot be quoted" is a prime example of the impact that change has on people who have been a part of an organization for a long time and are, perhaps, too comfortable with the status quo.

The church congregation in Florida that my husband, Ed, and I affiliated with had recently welcomed a new pastor. After we had been attending church services for several months, a long-serving member asked my husband what he thought about the new pastor and the direction the church was moving in under its new leadership. Without blinking an eye, Ed quickly responded, "Silence cannot be quoted."

When I asked Ed why he had responded in this rather strange and curious manner, he stated that followers must take special care not to prematurely evaluate a leadership context, and certainly not a new leader. He went on to say that it is not unusual for followers to be disturbed by the changes that a new leader makes ... changes that some might see as disrupting a very comfortable status quo. Ed added that new ideas often threaten followers who would much rather remain within their own comfort zones. The caution and care with which Ed responded to this long-time church member showed wisdom beyond measure. Ed was determined that he would not be guilty of reaching conclusions about both the church and the pastor that were premature, hasty, and therefore, patently unfair. My husband knew all too well the challenges that new leaders face. He was even more familiar with the challenges confronting transformative leaders because, for more than fourteen years, he had lived with one.

My spouse was correct in his caution to reserve making a judgment. He was wise in deciding to take time to observe how the leader handles both challenges and opportunities. This is a value understanding that must be held on both the transformative leader and those she or he wants to join them as transformation partners and collaborators. While this is true, it is still important to point out that the principal responsibility is on the transformative leader. Change can be disturbing. It brings with it uncertainty, especially if its bearer is an unknown commodity. Fortunately, change, innovation, and transformation are also exceedingly exciting and, when approached using appropriate steps, produce results that are willingly embraced and broadly celebrated.

Whenever a church (school or business) becomes stagnant, it loses its effectiveness. This is because organizations are designed to be vital. They are to be alive, and they are to be dynamic. They should evolve, grow, and change, or they will die. In order to maintain its life, a church (school or business) must continue to explore necessary change. Providing leadership for such change can be fairly easy, or it can be a thankless job. Within those churches where the pastor has a long tenure, his or her efforts to initiate change or even reexamination of current policies, philosophies, and processes have a much better chance of being positively received. This is largely because there is a track record. The clergyperson and those he or she leads have a shared history that any new pastor will not have the benefit of. However, this same longevity can also have a stymieing effect inasmuch as a pastor with a long-term history with an organization may himself or herself resist change precisely because it's safer not to change. The expression **"If it's not broke, don't fix it"** may well rule as the order of the day. In such instances, familiarity, comfort, and a long tenure with a church (school or business) become huge enemies to innovation, change, growth, and transformation.

It is doubtlessly true that newly selected church, school, or business leaders, especially when they are transformative in their worldview and behavior, are under constant scrutiny. This is the case within the church, at least until their parishioners feel that they have been sufficiently tried and tested. A track record has to be established with his or her congregants, students, employees and, invariably, this will take time. This trial period is particularly interesting because the need for organizational change is precisely why transformative leaders are hired over more traditional leaders. More and more, trustee committees, search committees, and governing boards are coming to accept that strategic organizational change is vital to the survival of theirs and every other organization. Increasingly, trustee committees, search committees, and governing boards understand that if they are to fulfill their missions, it will require achieving a balance between the status quo and strategic change.

On Becoming Visionary

Where there is no vision, the people perish.
Proverbs 29:18

To lead is to be courageous and open to change. The conversion experience and even the call that pastors receive is akin to an act of visionary leadership. Claiming the unknown through one's faith walk is a description of visionary leadership within a spiritual dimension. Many pastors describe their faith journey through a series of miracles that led them to the ministry. To be visionary means to walk by faith. It means remaining open and being receptive to that which cannot be seen. Jesus said it best when he repeatedly said to the disciples, "If you would only believe."

At a time when it is most needed, many of the members of our congregations are not applying their very powerful personal faith journeys to the churches where they serve. The result is that our congregations have been and will continue to suffer. Too often, the temptation is to become transformed through tradition and upward mobility. However, transformation and tradition are quite literally oxymoronic. To be transformed is to be liberated from traditional ways of thinking, seeing, and doing.

It is true that many seminaries do, in fact, teach courses in group dynamics that successfully prepare their ministerial students to serve their congregations. Only recently have these educational centers begun to examine leadership studies and the principles of the Caring Community beyond the traditional courses in administration and theology that are included in the curriculum. I applaud those seminaries that are beginning to prepare clergy for the twenty-first century challenges ... challenges that were not a part of the seminary curricula twenty or even ten years ago. Courses in group dynamics and transformative leadership are greatly needed as an important part of the preparation of the future leaders of church congregations. While seminarians discuss the discernment process throughout their studies and exploration into the ministry, the content of the academic curricula must reflect elements of the *affective domain* for a true exploration into visionary leadership.

The presence of courses related to human and group dynamics and transformative learning is refreshing because clergy and laity alike have been bound and held hostage to traditional practices and habits that have produced very disappointing results. Far too often, clergy and laity have feared making decisions that might disturb congregants who have been members of the church for many years and hold significant positions within the church. Many of these congregants are determined to preserve tradition and hold power close to their vests. Knowing that these same church elders will evaluate their performance and even make decisions about their tenure with the church, those clergy who might want to bring in innovation and change are effectively stopped. It does take courage to go against the status quo. It takes courage to challenge parishioners to take different approaches and positions that lead them to embrace missions and ministries that transform congregations first and then move outwardly to evangelize the unchurched.

I am often asked about where and how I became a visionary leader. The truth is, I have always been visionary but did not claim this gift because it was either not valued or readily recognized. I quite deliberately packaged my visionary qualities, and certainly my visionary zeal, in a way that would neither threaten nor confront the managers and traditionalists who were often the leaders or my bosses. In order to fit in and succeed, I hid my talents for too many years. I admired those who dared to claim their God-given talents as prodders, challengers, movers, and shakers. It was not until I assumed the role of a college president and CEO that I dared to model transformative leadership traits and skills. The word "visionary" means to move beyond traditional ways of thinking and doing in order to open a learning space where creativity and innovation become possible. More importantly, the word "visionary" means to open a learning space where the Holy Spirit is able to facilitate reflection and even change.

While it would have certainly not been consistent with my personality, it would have been far easier for me to assume the more traditional role of president and carry forth programs that were already in place than it was to ask the questions: What is missing? What is needed to respond to a hurting and hungry world? What should we be doing in addition to the mission? What do we think our community needs?

Because my approach was so markedly different from what others had observed, I was seen as someone who was just creating more work and, of course, stirring up things that were better off left alone. Some wondered why I was operating differently and instituting change so rapidly. I am pleased to tell you that at both institutions where I have served as president, stakeholders have and continue to describe innovations and changes as miracles. This was in the face of, and in spite of, many naysayers. I take no personal credit for doing more than allowing God to use me to open the door as a facilitator for new information, new insights, new actions, and for amazing outcomes to occur. My role as the facilitator is akin to that of clergy leaders and other organizational heads.

A Prayer for Discernment:
"Not my will, but thy will."

There is one critical point that must be made regarding taking risks. It is imperative that the facilitator have credibility either through the power made available to them through position or group sanctions. Too often, individuals become frustrated when they practice critical thinking and lead others to do the same. They are viewed as troublemakers. All effective organizations and their leaders must create spaces for prodding, questioning, listening, group reflection, and of course, prayer for discernment.

The discernment process is a rebirth and an awakening of the soul when individual's hearts are warmly touched. Rarely will we ever hear this process described as intellectually driven or motivated by logic. On the contrary, the conversion process is driven and facilitated by emotion that then generates attention from the logic domain. This being the case, it is important to declare that there are some practices within our churches that prevent the creation of a space for discernment. These practices simply do not allow for the occurrence of the conversion experience. Our churches are not growing because few people are having such experiences. The limited number of conversion experiences taking place within our churches is because the sermons and acts of worship are geared only toward the intellectual and logical domain. It is amazing how Jesus used parables to touch both the affective (heart) domain and the logical reasoning process in order that the conversion experience might be created. Just imagine hearing a parable that conflicts and challenges the traditions of your time. The parable takes you to a point where you are now in deep reflection. You have been touched by the lessons contained in the parable … lessons that have touched your heart and your head. As we look at the need to re-examine our assumptions, as well as our need to think outside of the box, I want to look at a typical Sunday worship service and critically analyze it for the many lessons found within.

While we have discussed the importance of sharing life experiences, storytelling, and mission outreach as facilitators into the spiritual domain, the church service should be instrumental in opening up this lens.

The men, women, and children who make up the membership of our churches are in need of leaders who are visionary … otherwise the people will surely perish. Leadership that is being called forth today must constantly pray to God for discernment in all matters. It is a prayer that grows out of our continued belief in the singular power of God and in God's unqualified love for those for whom he gave his life. It is a prayer that confirms our need to be guided by God lest we fall in a ditch and unless we be responsible for misguiding those we would lead. In the presence of the Holy Spirit through discernment, transformation that is guided and blessed is assured. Discernment may come through our prayers, acts of devotion to God, listening with our hearts, community dialogue and reflection, mission outreach, and hopefully, from our worship services.

I submit to you that it is resistance to change and resistance to being transformed that are killing traditional mainline churches rather than any willful intention on the part of the leadership of charismatic churches to systematically siphon off membership. To think otherwise is to compare this "logic" to the young teenager who is in love but loses the object of his affection when someone else "steals" his sweetheart. Just as the teenager finally matures enough to discover that it was not possible to lose something he never really had, the church serving the twenty-first century congregant must understand that having a member who attends service regularly, tithes, and works on committees or auxiliaries is not a guarantee that he or she will not go elsewhere. The truth is that people go where they are fed spiritually, emotionally, and educationally. They go where they can meet the Holy Spirit. If they are questioned about their experience, they speak about the power of Scripture and its connection to their current day realities. The sermon connects to their hearts and not just the intellect. It is very unfortunate that too many of our congregations never open up hearts. They fail to activate the spiritual dimension and leave members feeling empty and isolated. There is something almost magical about feeling the spirit of God as it also connects you with every person alive. When this happens, we feel a strong connection to God as we are touched by the Holy Spirit. What is not clear is whether our churches are in essence blocking discernment.

Blocking discernment is an affront to God. It is a gift that is given to those who seek God. Through God, discernment is made possible. Discernment requires receptivity, prayer, listening, reflecting, searching, questioning, and of course, yielding one's will and false sense of power to God. It also requires courage and self-examination. Often the needed change that must occur starts with the leadership. Music, sermons, Scripture lessons, and Bible studies can create the reflection that is necessary for yielding our will to that of God's. If traditional churches became keen observers of today's charismatic churches, they would discover clergypeople using Scripture and storytelling as powerful tools to tap the spiritual domain of learning. They would discover churches that have put aside certain traditions and rituals in order to get to the business of bringing people to the Communion table.

The Sacred Hour

The Sunday worship hour is holy and is another lens into the spiritual domain. It is perhaps the one time that many Christians stop to focus exclusively on God as the author and finisher of their faith. It is the one time that many among the ranks of the unsaved might enter the house of God. And yet, I regularly observe congregations interrupting the spirit of the worship hour with announcements and other traditional rituals. Admittedly, this has been the practice for too many years to count. However, it is extremely important to understand that traditional church rituals, such as making announcements and recognizing visitors within this sacred time, interferes with congregants' communing with the Holy Spirit. It's interesting how churches invite the Holy Spirit to "stop by here" but then get busy blocking the Holy Spirit's arrival by focusing attention on church picnics, Women's Day meetings, choir or praise dance rehearsals, and news of trips to other churches. Through these and other announcements, the focus of the worship service is taken off God and redirected to individual members of the church (i.e., specific deacon or deaconess, head of a ministry, etc.). Inadvertently, the church has created competition between individual church members and God. This is not a choice that congregants have entered God's house church to make.

Once the worship service begins, the church's one and only goal should be facilitating each member's movement toward communion with God ... doing all that can be done to reach the point where every single parishioner's heart is touched as they are given opportunities for reflection through scripture and the word. This requires the uninterrupted flow of music, Scripture, sermon, testimonies, and acts of evangelism. Adequate time must be devoted to these four levels of worship without interruption. Or to put it another way, it is only through the spiritual domain of learning (touching the heart) that communion with God becomes manifest. I have had the experience of meeting the Holy Spirit through music only to have my communion with the Spirit abruptly cut short by an unexpected change in tempo, signaling movement into the next scripted phase of the service. I admit there are many traditions and rituals that are sacred and need to be respected so long as they do not impede mission and ministry. However, the goal of the worship experience is to facilitate communion with the Holy Spirit ... to transform church into vital places of worship and transformation.

The greatest process used for facilitating communion with the Holy Spirit and thereby touching hearts is through storytelling and music. It is also critical that Scripture be brought to life within a context that reflects our life and times. If the conversion experience is the work of God, how often do leaders block the movement through other rituals and practices? Are clergy prepared to carry the burden of permitting environments to exist that keep their congregants from the Holy Spirit ... having them depart feeling further away than they felt upon entering the sanctuary?

Many mainline denominations are questioning why charismatic churches are growing by leaps and bounds while their own churches are shrinking. Leaders of these mainstream churches that have lost portions of their memberships to more charismatic churches have been known to confront these pastors, charging them with "stealing their members." Nothing could be further from the truth. My experience is that people go where they are being fed and nurtured in spirit ... where they are being nourished through Scripture ... where communion with the Holy Spirit is more the rule then it is an exception. Charismatic churches have leaders who speak the language of the people. It is a language that is alive and that breathes life into those who hear it. It is about storytelling that is tied back to Scripture. After all, Jesus taught through parables that created easy opportunities to reflect on and exit from traditional ways of thinking and acting. Perhaps these congregations are growing because the sacred hour is not interrupted. It is continuous from the moment of prayer, Scripture, the word, and an offering of the collection plate for some just cause. While the fellowship hour should not be abruptly interwoven into a time that should be devoted exclusively to God, this does not minimize the importance of emphasis that should be placed on the development and sustaining of Caring Communities. Instead, this observation suggests that if the focus remains on a continuous praise and thanksgiving to God, people in the membership would be moved toward the spiritual dimension. Just sit and observe your congregation and see the disconnection as soon as a person gets us to read announcements related to events occurring during the week. You will observe a disconnection from the sacred hour to a secular focus on individuals versus God. There is a need to focus on the local church community needs, but perhaps the time should be in advance of the church service or following closure of that hour.

As I think about the kinds of things that result in members leaving mainstream churches for charismatic churches, I am reminded of a variety of things that block discernment and, of course, grieve the Holy Spirit. They make transformation impossible.

Many churches do not realize that conflicts exist because the congregation is not vital and not fully motivated or devoted to the mission at hand. When congregations place their focus on the sacred hour and sustaining Caring Communities, they can avoid such conflicts as infighting, domination by a few members, mistrust, and the decline in church membership.

If you want to find a dying church, it will be one that is consumed with infighting and tugs of war. Infighting occurs when there is a false sense of power and when the ego opposes God. Many people leave congregations because a few people dominate, control, and judge harshly those who do not conform or agree with them. Unfortunately, even some pastors and laity are capable of leading this harmful leadership charge. Congregations that might be called vital are much more focused on service and mission and have little time to engage in infighting and nonproductive actions. Vital congregations use their time and energy to do God's work without worrying about who gets credit, who is more visible, or who has the power.

Committee meetings that take place in dying churches have congregants who feel that some of the church's leaders hold others hostage through controlling actions, disregarding participation and input, and blocking ideas. In essence, these are church leaders who call their meetings "open" while their actions might as well post a sign that says "Not Welcome." Within a vital congregation, all members and pastors model behavior that communicates that Christ is center.

As a university professor with a background in adult education and sociology, I am keenly aware of just how damaging it can be to hold on to assumptions. I've seen classroom teachers, as well as college and university administrators, make far too many assumptions about the students they teach and/or interact with. Today's students are very different than my own generation of student peers and many other previous generations of students. The challenges today's students face are enormous. As young people out of school for the summer, our concern was more about which summer program we wanted to apply for than it was about how to successfully compete with full-time permanent employees who are anxious to work additional hours to cover rising fuel costs and weekly increases in food prices. At school, we were concerned that our lockers might be broken into and not whether or not we might end up like one of the twenty-nine students in Chicago's school district who died from in-school violence! We worried about syphilis and gonorrhea, both of which could be treated with penicillin. Today's students are also faced with AIDS, a continuously mutating virus that has killed more than 25 million people since 1981 and that, more than twenty years since the first case was recorded in Los Angeles, is still without a cure. The lives of today's students are racked with increased crime, homelessness, abandonment, abuse, and myriad other problems and issues … problems and issues that overwhelm countless older adults.

A student at my university was experiencing a variety of challenges. Stepping outside of the box and casting off assumptions, we looked further and allowed ourselves to remain open to the possibilities. What we found was heart-wrenching for this was a homeless college student … a young person who was determined to earn a college degree but who literally lived in his old car. When asked whether his parents could help, we learned that not one but both parents were incarcerated. We often point to such tangibles as professionally styled hair and nails or designer jeans and jewelry. We lament that in the presence of these things, some of these same students complain there is no money to purchase textbooks. We quickly embrace assumptions that seem to be supported by the tangible things … by the things that we can see. But these tangibles are like plugs in a hole-filled dam. Always under enormous unseen pressures, the dams of our students' lives are, more times than not, just a plug away from bursting and washing away every hope and every dream.

I am reminded of a heart-wrenching story one of my faculty members shared with me about her encounter with a student several years ago. This was an enormously powerful experience and one that, according to the professor, will not ever be forgotten. On what seemed a rather ordinary day, the professor recalled passing a female student as she was leaving the ladies' rooms on campus. As she exited the restroom, a female student entered and, as was her habit, she spoke. The student was not enrolled in a class with the professor but did have a brother who was. Apparently, the professor had previously been introduced to this female student by her brother. This was how she recognized her. She did not recall the student's name, but for the sake of this retelling, I will refer to the student as Joan.

Apparently, as Joan entered the restroom, the professor greeted her and then asked how she was. Joan said that she was fine, however, according to the professor she did not sound fine. The professor shared with me that she heard that still small voice saying to her, "You need to turn around and go back into the rest room and you need to do it now!" She did and stood face-to-face with a student who was totally demoralized. She shared with me that Joan was hurt and sad. She was despondent and, quite literally, said that she had had enough! During the professor's conversation with Joan, she learned that since the start of the semester in August, Joan had had three roommates. The first roommate had moved out after running up a telephone bill of more than $700. The second roommate had left, taking all of Joan's electronic equipment with her: her television, stereo, and microwave. The professor went on to say that Joan was now living with a third roommate and had just had about all she could take. According to the professor, Joan was "sick and tired of being sick and tired."

To the professor, this student sounded suicidal, and understandably, she was alarmed. It was very close to the Thanksgiving break, and because the holiday break was just a few days away, the professor asked Joan whether she was going home. She talked with me about how unprepared she was to hear Joan say that she planned to remain in town and on campus during the break. It was clear to the professor that Joan needed to go home. She needed to be with family, with people whom she loved and who loved her back in healthy and, even more importantly, in healing ways. I am proud to say that this was precisely what the professor told the student. She told her that sometimes you just need to lie at the foot of your mother or grandmother's bed for a while. You don't even have to say anything; you just need to be able to lie there.

Joan took the professor's advice and did go home over the Thanksgiving weekend. The professor shared with me that shortly after the break, she and Joan's paths crossed. They happened to run into each other just as they had that fateful morning. According to the professor, she saw and heard a completely different student. She first noticed Joan's smile and then saw that Joan seemed confident and assured as she stood and talked with her. She was better.

I prefer not to think about what the end might have been for this young woman if the professor had withheld her response based on assumptions she held about the way that Joan said that she was "fine." She could have said that Joan was being rude; that Joan was just distracted; that she had boyfriend problems; that whatever was wrong wasn't her business. Joan's "fine" and unspoken words along with nonverbal clues had opened up the affective domain of learning—the professor's heart—and she responded just as she should have, just as Joan needed her to and just as God was calling her to.

Once I understood the spiritual power involved in accessing the affective domain of learning, I came to better understand my new role as an advocate for transformative leading and transformative leadership. As I taught in the area of transformative leadership at one United Methodist Seminary and several colleges, I found my "home" as a visionary leader and change agent. On a daily basis, the Holy Spirit spoke to me about the tremendous value of my research findings and how they were inseparable from transformation. The Holy Spirit convinced me of my moral obligation to move quickly forward to design and institute new ways of preparing leaders to serve churches, schools, and businesses that were stagnant and in jeopardy of dying.

Paul on the Road to Damascus: A Significant Emotional Experience

For Christians, we understand this theological characterization because throughout the Gospel, Jesus transformed those who followed him. To be a believer in Christ was, in fact, to be transformed. The most dramatic biblical example of this was the transformation of Saul into Paul on the road to Damascus. Knocked from his horse, Paul could no longer see. He could only listen to God's voice, but as he was led into Damascus, he knew that he was undergoing a transformation. Even Paul's question, "Who are you, Lord?" suggests that he knew with whom he was having the encounter. With the answer, "I am Jesus, whom you are persecuting. It is hard for you, this kicking against the goad," the affective domain was accessed. Pollock writes about Paul's transformation saying:

> Then Paul knew. In a second that seemed an eternity he saw the wounds in Jesus' hands and feet, saw the face and knew that he has seen the Lord, that he was alive as Stephen and the others had said, and that he loved not only those whom Paul persecuted but *Paul*: It is hard for *you* to kick against the goad. Not one word of reproach.

Pollock continues about Paul:

> Paul had never admitted to himself that he had felt pricks of a goad as he raged against Stephen and his disciples. But now, instantaneously, he was shatteringly aware that he has been fighting Jesus. And fighting himself, his conscience, his powerlessness, the darkness and chaos in his soul. God hovered over this chaos and brought him to the moment of new creation. It wanted only his "Yes."

The power of the transformation that becomes possible might be lost to the reader without what has always been for me a very powerful story. The story is told of a father who had two sons. He loved being a father. He loved his sons. The neighborhood expression, "When you see one, you see the other two," was a consistent refrain. They were always together, always going and coming. He taught them to ride their bikes, to throw and catch a football, to fish, and drive a car. He taught them how to knot a tie and how to change a tire. The hours he spent talking to them about setting goals and making plans for their futures, establishing priorities, keeping promises, and always doing the right thing were too many to count. They were his classroom, and he was their teacher. He was a dream of a father.

Directly across the street from this father and his two sons lived a single mother. She also had a son, and he, too, was always coming and always going. The only difference was that he was always alone. He pretty much raised himself while his mother struggled to keep food in the refrigerator and the landlord at bay. Time moved along for both families and all three of the boys grew up. Because the father insisted that his two sons study and prioritize properly, both boys earned academic scholarships. They completed college and, because they grew to love their college towns and friends, limited their visits home to the holidays and family emergencies.

It was Thanksgiving week, and the sons were both home. Dinner was over and, stuffed, they decided to walk through the neighborhood where they lived for the first eighteen years of their lives. Shortly after they left the house, the sound of gunfire was heard in the distance and then running footsteps, followed by loud banging on the front door. A long-time neighbor and friend came running in, yelling for the father to come fast. He did and, approaching a small side street, stopped in his tracks as he realized that his two sons lay on the ground in front of him. They were both dead, shot and killed by the boy who lived directly across the street. How might the lives of these two families have been changed? How might this story have ended if, through all those years of coming and going with his two sons, the father had simply walked a few more steps across to the house directly in front of his own and said, "Come go with us." How positive a turn his life might have taken!

I am enormously moved every single time I hear this story recounted. It pulls at my heart strings and compels me to say that this must never happen again. Because I have been changed, my question becomes, "What is my role in making sure that it doesn't?" My research was really about changes brought on by significant emotional experiences not unlike that of the father who lost his two sons at the hands of another's son whose classroom became the darker side of life.

It is virtually impossible for the human heart, made by God himself, to remain detached and unfeeling in the presence of such stories as a loving father's discovery that both of his sons had been murdered while taking a walk after Thanksgiving dinner, or a co-ed who has reached the end of her rope and talks about things not being worth it and having had enough, or a young girl running to catch a man who received only her anger and contempt while trying to sell pencils to relieve his hunger. An inventory of these experiences has demonstrated that prior held assumptions can be transformed (Preciphs 1989). It is provided for the reader in the Appendices.

Transformation can occur from both positive and negative significant emotional experiences. People respond to the changes that they observe in others in a variety of ways. Granted, change should be expected when people are placed in different environments in order to take advantage of new or additional opportunities. When people volunteer, they are often changed by their volunteer experiences. However, it is the unanticipated and unexpected change that most often causes people to be no longer at ease. This was the change that made those who returned from their volunteer experiences now seem so different.

As a university president, I interact with many of the 3,000-plus students on my campus. I am perpetually intrigued about their change process ... that as juniors and seniors they look and sound very different from their freshman and sophomore years. It is important students understand that they are, in fact, expected to change. They are supposed to be transformed by four years of higher education; to resist this change is to disappoint and disillusion family, friends, peers, and most especially, themselves.

There is a wonderful daily devotional called "Streams in the Desert" which, in addition to prayer, is a wonderful way to begin each day. In one of the daily devotions, the author, L. B. Cowan, relates the story of one of the world's most skilled lapidaries, who was charged with cutting a magnificent newly discovered diamond. After months of studying the gem, the lapidary was ready to begin his work which, to the shock and dismay of onlookers, involved first striking a blow to the surface of the diamond. To the untrained eye, the lapidary's blow to the gem appeared reckless, wasteful, and without logic. However, the lapidary did precisely what was needed to be done to transform the one stone into two diamonds that were perfect in their shapeliness and radiance. The skilled eye of the lapidary saw what was accessible only because he was willing to cut through and go beyond what was readily visible to get to what was not. What would have become of the diamond had it resisted its own transformation? In this same devotion, Cowan speaks about the human propensity to resist the process of transformation that

God ordains as the vehicle through which we are to draw closer to him and says of our all to frequent resistance to change, "He is making you now and you are quarreling with the process" (Cowan 1996).

Transformative leadership involves a process that might be uncomfortable for the overwhelming number of us. In large part, this is because as formally trained clergypeople, members of the academy, and leaders in business and industry, we are much more at home with that which begins and most often ends with research and subsequently the thinking and actions that emerge from our use of academic sources. However, rather than traditional methods and approaches, it is transformative thinking—thinking outside of the box—that leads us into the world of the lapidary who sees that the uncut gem's greatest value is in its unseen possibilities.

Like the lapidary's newly cut gem, volunteers who served these three national agencies of The United Methodist Church for a year were, in fact, transformed in ways that were totally unexpected. When they returned to their home conferences, they were simply different than peers who had remained behind. Because their once conservative views were now more liberal, they were no longer viewed as representatives of the local areas that had originally elected them for membership. Not surprisingly, the transformation in those returning to their home conferences was not received well. To say that they were surprised would be an understatement.

They could have learned something from Paul. While he was unprepared for the response of the Gentiles, Paul was not surprised. In his persecution of the Gentiles, Paul was zealous and sincerely believed that he was doing God's will. Pollock writes that in Damascus, Paul "charged forward with the same vehemence and abandon that he charged into his persecution" (Pollock). Instead of a disciple, the Gentiles saw in Paul a turncoat. Instead of being convinced of Paul's transformation, they were angry. As convinced as Paul was that his persecution of the Gentiles was ordered by God so now was he certain, beyond any doubt, that Jesus Christ was Lord of his life. The new and more liberal views of the returning volunteers were also unanticipated and became a source of dissonance between themselves and their local counterparts, who now characterized them as "radicals."

At this juncture, it is important to remember there is a marked difference between *transformative leadership* and *indoctrination*. This was an important finding in my own study because of the relative ease in using transformative learning for purposes of indoctrination. While transformative learning allows the individual to search for the truth, the goal of indoctrination is to manipulate in order to ensure a predetermined outcome. In my view, this is a call for those churches, schools, and businesses that seek to employ the transformative learning and transformative leadership paradigm to ground their programs in the study of ethics. Such leadership programs also study those people who dare to dream and vision.

What I've learned about transformation is that this process is capable of shifting value systems and lifelong beliefs not solely through critical thinking, but mostly because our hearts are touched. When this happens, a learning space is created just long enough for self and group reflection for deep searching of new truths that may emerge. This is what the spreading of the Gospel meant for the transformation of nations and the world.

Chapter III

Dr. Mary Mcleod Bethune

The Story Of A Remarkable Twentieth Century Transformative Leader

It is a profound act of God's ongoing Covenant with Dr. Mary McLeod Bethune that she founded and nurtured Bethune-Cookman University as a Caring Community that extended far into the community for both African Americans and whites. Bethune-Cookman University is a place where Bethune entrusted her legacy of civic engagement and social responsibility. She challenged a nation to move away from systems of oppression to opportunities of hope. She placed service above self and, today, is seen as one of the greatest role models of transformative leadership of the twentieth century. Dr. Bethune is one of the best examples of a transformative leader. Her story supports the formation of Caring Communities, which she established and sustained through town hall meetings and convocations that were powerful and emotional stimulants for her students and the community. Her witness to the process of transformation also demonstrates the use of the spiritual domain.

The life of Mary McLeod Bethune is nothing short of extraordinary. Hers is a story that continues to fascinate and inspire generation after generation. It is the story of a woman who from a young child was blessed with the kind of faith that does, in fact, move mountains. Mary McLeod Bethune's faith produced the results that Jesus alluded to when he repeatedly admonished the disciples with the words, "If you would only believe." She did believe and, with holy boldness, she moved through her life with vigor and a conviction that remains difficult to find the words for.

Mary McLeod Bethune: The Woman, Her Calling, Her Legacy

Mary McLeod Bethune's extraordinary life began just on the other side of American slavery. Both of her parents had been slaves. Some accounts report that she was the last of their seventeen children and the only one born free, while other studies tell us that she was the fifteenth of seventeen and the first to be born outside of slavery. What we know for sure is that her July 10, 1875, birth in Mayesville, Georgia, occurred just twelve short years after the Emancipation Proclamation was signed. Bethune and her siblings held the truly extraordinary distinction of all having the same biological parents. And even though many of the children lived on other plantations, Bethune's parents, Patsy and Samuel, lived as husband and wife on the same plantation.

When slavery ended, Bethune's parents set as a goal to reclaim all of their children that they might live together as an intact family. The value of family and the commitment to high morals were deeply woven into Bethune's personality and, indeed, her psyche by both of her parents. No doubt Bethune's knowledge that her mother bore a large burn on her chest as a consequence of fighting off the sexual advances of her master's son went far in communicating the importance of self-respect and the high moral standard by which she led her own life.

Bethune was always older than her years. Biographies discuss her emergence as a leader, first among her siblings, even though she was far from being the oldest. Her willingness to step out in front was interesting for a number of reasons, with the most significant of them being that she was dark-skinned and had very pronounced African features ... features that, during most of her eighty years, were considered a disadvantage to access power and privilege.

There is no doubt that many events worked together to shape Bethune's life and journey. She learned about hard work as a child by working ten to twelve hours a day in the cotton fields on land her parents farmed as sharecroppers. She learned that desire means nothing unless you are willing to work by putting one step in front of the other as she made the ten-mile trip to and from school each day up until the sixth grade. Sadly, Bethune's move toward continuing her education was abruptly stopped because money that might have been used to pay for additional study had to be rerouted when the family's mule died.

In 1887, a gift of a scholarship to Scotia Seminary in North Carolina answered the McLeod family's prayers when, after learning about the work being done in South Carolina to educate black children, a white Quaker woman, Mary Chrisman from Denver, Colorado, sent news that she was willing to help in the education of a black female. Many years later, Bethune wrote, "To this day, my heart thrills with gratitude at the memory of that day when a poor dressmaker, sewing for her daily bread, heard my call and came to my assistance. Out of her scanty earnings, she invested in a life—my life!" Bethune understood how terrible it is to have your fate decided for you by someone else, and a variety of experiences is pivotal in shaping and molding Bethune's vision and passion for change.

While visiting the plantation where her parents were once slaves, a white child offered to let Bethune look at a "picture" book because she knew that Bethune couldn't read and wasn't ever likely to be able to do so in the future. Needless to say, this experience ignited Bethune's resolve to become a truly educated member of her race. There is no doubt that one of the most harrowing experiences to happen to Bethune took place when she and her father went to town to sell the produce they had grown on their leased farm. Standing outside of the store, they witnessed a white man hold a candle so close to the face of a black man that he responded quickly and quite naturally by promptly pushing the hand away. The push caused the man to lose balance, and unable to catch himself, he fell to the ground. A white observer immediately yelled for a rope, and within minutes the man's life was over!

In 1894, Bethune left Scotia after seven years and, with a scholarship to attend the Dwight Moody Institute for Home and Foreign Missions and the continued assistance of Mary Chrisman, headed for Chicago. It would be an understatement to say that she was in the minority. In fact, she was the sole minority student. Out of 1,000 students, only Bethune was black. While Bethune's upbringing did not prepare her for every slight or discriminatory act she encountered, it did instill in her a clear sense of pride for who she was and an appreciation for diversity. Even though the legal end to segregation was three quarters of a century away, black and white sharecroppers and farmers came together at the McLeod's farm for "moonlight" parties where celebrating an end to the hard labor that was a constant part of their lives took precedence over keeping the races separate. Blacks and whites also came together to help bring in the harvest for their former slave masters and, ignoring racial differences, together celebrated the end of the farming season at hog-killing parties. No doubt, these types of interactions served Bethune well as she interacted with whites at the Moody Institute.

One of the desires that Bethune carried with her to Moody Institute was that of traveling to Africa to work as a missionary ... a fire that had been ignited under her after listening to the traveling preachers who routinely stopped for fellowship at her parents' home during their travels. Inherently, Bethune understood the interconnectedness of the members of the human family. It was logical then that she would make her fervent desire to travel to Africa known after the completion of her formal study at the Moody Institute.

Following Bethune's formal study at the Moody Institute, she asked to go to Africa as a missionary and was soundly turned down. It is difficult to describe what must have been tremendous heartache and enormous disappointment at being told there were no opportunities for blacks to go to Africa as missionaries. It seems to me it was something of an oxymoron to contemplate that there were no opportunities for blacks to work as missionaries in black Africa.

It has been said that some things happen so that others things become possible. While we will never know what would have been the end had Bethune been allowed to go to Africa as a missionary, what we do know is that this closed door lead to the opening of another door—a door that led to the most important phase of her life and a legacy replete with presidents, first ladies, presidential cabinet appointments, ambassadorships, and the founding of a university that in 1904 began with five girls and in 2008 has more than 3,000 students.

The Answered Prayer of a Dream

> And Jabez called on the God of Israel saying, "Oh, that you would bless me indeed and enlarge my territory, that your hand would be with me, and that you would keep me from evil, that I may not cause pain!" So God granted him what he requested.
>
> 1 Chronicles 4:10

And so it was with Bethune that God did, in fact, enlarge her territory. After leaving Moody Institute in Chicago, Bethune went to Palatka, Florida, where she started a community school, talked with sawmill workers, and spent time visiting youth clubs and those who were incarcerated. Five years after she first arrived in Palatka, one of the local ministers, a Reverend Pratt, suggested to Bethune that Daytona Beach offered a unique opportunity to put her many ideas about educating black children into practice (Long 2004). In Daytona, the railroad was being built, and black workers were moving into the area with their families, most of whom had children and not a single school to send them to. With the faith of Abraham, Bethune left the west coast of the state and headed to Daytona Beach, destined to forever impact, influence, and to bring change to the lives of countless young people, their families, their communities, Florida, and the nation.

If you were to ask anyone who knows anything at all about the institution that Mary McLeod Bethune started in October 1904, almost to the person, you will hear the constant refrain that she began her school with "a dollar and fifty cents, five little girls, and faith in God ..." the substance of things hoped for and the evidence of things not seen.

Bethune possessed a completely uncompromising belief that God was not a respecter of people, that he did not discriminate, and that through him all things were possible. While outward appearances were that she arrived in Daytona Beach alone, with neither money nor connections, the truth was that she arrived with more than enough. She was the possessor of a powerful dream, a dream that had its very foundation in God's grace and mercy, a dream that Bethune constantly nourished through her relationship with the Holy Spirit. And so she began.

In 1904, Bethune located and rented a two-room building from one of the city's few black landowners. The first desks she and her students used were packing crates that had been discarded at the local dump. Additional crates and other items were donated by the community's other black residents. While always grateful for every contribution, Bethune knew that she would have to do a lot more, or progress toward the realization of her school would continue to be painstakingly slow. She walked or rode her bike from house to house, where she courageously knocked on doors, told the occupants about her school, and asked them to help her.

Dr. Bethune spoke with what is so often referred to in our churches as holy boldness. I like that term, and in my view, no person has demonstrated and reflected it more in their life's work than Mary McLeod Bethune. It took holy boldness to go to Palatka and holy boldness to leave after five years to come to Daytona Beach; holy boldness to place five dollars in change on a table as the down payment on the $250 piece of property that would become the permanent school; and holy boldness to go door-to-door asking whites for help to build a school for black girls at a time when African American women in the South were nonentities to be used or ignored—"the mule of the world," as writer Alice Walker's now-classic phrase asserts.

It was this same holy boldness, undergirded by her indomitable faith, that led Bethune to pen a letter to the owner of Cincinnati-headquartered Proctor and Gamble, James Gamble. History reports that Gamble agreed to the meeting, never imagining that the well-written letter had been authored by a black woman.

Just as historical accounts consistently articulate the founding of Bethune's school with "a dollar and fifty cents, five little girls, and faith in God," accounts also consistently talk about Bethune's first encounter with James Gamble. Once again stepping out on faith, Bethune went right to the heart of the matter. Almost immediately, she asked Gamble if he would agree to serve on the board of her school. No doubt surprised by the request, Gamble wanted Bethune to give him a good reason for agreeing to the request and is reported to have said to her, "Why should I share in such a venture?"

The truth is, Dr. Bethune really didn't want Gamble to serve on the board of her school. What she wanted was for Gamble to share in a dream. Her response to him—"Because I'm not asking you to chair a school board; I'm asking you to chair a dream"—proved to be an exceedingly persuasive response. The affective domain was accessed, and Gamble was moved! For fifteen years, James Gamble served as Bethune's chairman of the board, using his influence to attract countless supporters and benefactors.

Bethune's decision to write to James Gamble asking for a meeting to speak with him about her vision was not unlike Nehemiah's decision to share with King Artaxerx the heaviness of his own heart as he thought of the destruction of the wall that surrounded Jerusalem, the city of his birth. In the instance of Nehemiah, Scripture says, "Then the king said unto me, 'For what dost thou make request?'" (Nehemiah 2:4). To Bethune's plea, Gamble offered a similar response asking, "Why should I share in such a venture?" When Bethune spoke of sharing in a dream, Gamble heard her with his heart and not just his intellect. Like King Artaxerx, Gamble heard both pain and passion through the unbridled lament, and like King Artaxerx, Gamble extended himself, making his resources available and clearing the way to provide what was needed to begin the important work of rebuilding—a wall in one instance and a people in the other.

Gamble's decision to put his support and significant influence behind Bethune was yet another confirmation of God's hand on Bethune's dream. The societal and racial realities of that period in American history suggested that Bethune's request was presumptuous, unrealistic, and surely out of season. Everything pointed to Gamble saying no that he was not interested and certainly not willing to get involved at the level Bethune requested. Instead, he said yes.

Mary McLeod Bethune was before her time. She saw things that never were and got busy developing relationships and working with others to make them so. In her way of thinking, the only barriers to realizing hopes and dreams were those that were self-imposed. Just thirty-nine years "up from slavery," Bethune showed a resolve and a tenacity to create a better life for blacks and, indeed, a better world, one issue at a time. She always moved outside of the proverbial box, flinging far and wide the traditional and, from the perspectives of almost everyone, the safer ways of thinking. She embraced the role of change agent and held a fervent belief that institutions of higher education have a moral obligation to act as agents for social change ,and while many might have seen her race and gender as obstacles to reaching her goals, she certainly did not.

As an agent of innovation and social change, Bethune saw no limits to addressing the disparities, inconsistencies, and challenges of which blacks were the constant targets and victims. Long, one of Bethune's more recent biographers, provides an exceptional example. She tells the story of one of Bethune's students becoming acutely ill. A ruptured appendix was the diagnosis. Then as now, an appendectomy was the only medical treatment. However, the sole hospital in Daytona Beach would not admit Bethune's student, who was sure to die without the surgery. Always one to see past obstacles and barriers into the potential and possibilities of all things, Bethune persuaded one of the hospital's staff doctors, Dr. C. C. Bohannon, to perform the surgery. The question of where to perform the procedure loomed. After some discussion with hospital officials, Dr. Bohannon was allowed to perform the operation in the screened-in porch located on the back of the hospital.

In the absence of a nurse of either race, Bethune worked as Dr. Bohannon's surgical assistant during the procedure. Despite delays in beginning the appendectomy and the less than ideal surgical environment, the procedure went well for Bethune's student. As you have no doubt concluded, the white hospital's refusal to serve black patients, even in life and death situations was, for Bethune, a harrowing and totally unacceptable situation. Her dissatisfaction was so great that Bethune's response was also immediate. She would build a hospital, but it would be a hospital that would serve everyone, regardless of race. Locating a room near the school, Bethune started her hospital with only two beds. In 1912, there were twenty-six beds, and the McLeod Hospital and Training School for Nurses was opened to serve all races (Long 2004).

It should come as no surprise that the hospital Bethune founded was intended to be used by all of Daytona's citizenry. Bethune meant for the entire community to benefit from its presence. She was committed to serving the community in all the ways and opportunities God presented. That God's hand was on Bethune is without question. He was blessing her indeed. Through Bethune's ability to bring together different constituencies to talk about what was needed to solve problems that concerned the entire community, God was, in fact, enlarging her territory.

Without question, the most frequently talked about forum for these discussions were the town-hall meetings—a vehicle she wisely used for building a Caring Community. Usually held on Sunday afternoons, these meetings allowed blacks and whites the opportunity to interact with each other in positive ways at a time when it was unheard for them to engage in significant dialogue about issues that mattered to both races. It simply didn't happen. Within the context of Bethune's town hall meetings, the issue of race was minimized as blacks and whites learned to appreciate diversity and accept differences while unwittingly availing themselves to the processes of *emancipatory learning*.

It was during these Sunday gatherings that blacks and whites shared with each other their own stories and their own very personal experiences, stories and experiences that caused unexpected reflection and a critical examination of deeply held assumptions. Through storytelling and sharing personal experiences, Bethune had effectively accessed the "affective domain of learning" and produced in each race the same kind of *significant emotional experiences* that the volunteers with the Methodist church had experienced and, I suspect, Jim, the transformed attorney mentioned earlier, had also experienced. A far mightier hand was at work, moving blacks and whites toward the only place where change became possible: the heart.

Bethune was extraordinarily effective in her analysis of the needs of a civic culture and sought to maximize the participation of all members of the community. She decried superficial analyses of the challenges faced by participatory democracies. Though she was solidly aware of and concerned about racial inequality, she was also keenly aware of the connections between various types of marginalization and oppression. She was enormously sensitive to the fact that the marginalization of any group of citizens—whether on the basis of gender, class, economic status, or any other stigmatized difference—was the nemesis to the very delicate fabric of a civic society and, even more importantly, God's will for all of God's people.

Bethune's commitment to bringing together and working with society's diverse populations, marginalized and otherwise, regardless of gender, class, or economic status, is evidenced in the varied nature of the many organizations she either founded or devoted her time and energies to. Bethune also helped integrate women into the military. A servant to all of humanity, she founded at least a half dozen organizations, including a women's advisory group composed of many of Daytona Beach's influential white women. Almost one hundred years later, the Women's Advisory Board continues to function as an important support auxiliary for the institution.

In 1935, Bethune founded the National Council of Negro Women and, in 2007, the organization has college, university, and general membership chapters throughout the United States. Bethune was also actively involved with American Red Cross in spite of blacks not being among those individuals and families who could avail themselves of the organization's emergency services. No stranger to being first or being the only black woman, Bethune was the only black woman at the founding meeting of the United Nations and United Negro College Fund. She was a personal friend to both Eleanor and President Franklin Roosevelt and served as an advisor to the Roosevelt White House. Dr. Bethune was appointed director of African American Affairs for the National Youth Administration by President Roosevelt under the auspices of the New Deal Works Progress Administration, and provided leadership for all of America's young people—so God granted her what she requested for she had a vision.

Today, our founder is an international leadership icon. She lived and worked to democratize society through transformative models of education that few others understood. She was ahead of her time as a social justice advocate, leader, educator, and political figure. More importantly, she was a woman of God who had devoted her entire life to young people and community empowerment. Dr. Bethune was a model for transformative leadership, a term as yet uncoined and, unfortunately, still not fully understood.

Dr. Bethune understood that mission work through volunteerism created opportunities for embracing one's heart, which eventually reached the head. Dr. Bethune started Bethune-Cookman University with a $1.50, five little girls, and faith in God. So in touch was she with the heart's place of prominence that the official seal designed for the college in 1904 depicts a circle divided into sections labeled "Hand" (for service), "Head" (for intellectual pursuits), and "Heart" (for the affective domain of values and emotions). Until recently, many alumni did not fully understand what she meant by heart, but they are beginning to see the true educator/leader through the lens of transformative learning and leadership. When influential leaders around the world worked with Dr. Bethune, they looked beyond race and gender because she was one of the few African Americans of her time period who was successful in shifting paradigms based on transformative learning.

Her service benefited people from Haiti to the Bahamas and other nations that had little understanding of the racial divide in our country.

A Lifetime of Learning and Growing through Service

Although not called service learning during her time, Dr. Bethune fully understood the process needed to challenge our traditionally held assumptions. It is a process that requires that we be present and that we show up in order to engage others and in order to be engaged by others in ways that are reciprocal and mutually rewarding. It is a process that seeks to draw upon us as facilitators while recognizing and respecting the intrinsic value of community residents as facilitators in their own right.

Dr. Bethune understood that she could transcend both real and imagined differences in race and gender by utilizing service learning as a lens that facilitated self-discovery and, thereby, a deeper understanding and a more honest critique of society's flaws. It was through this up close and very personal interaction with "the other" that Dr. Bethune inspired people to seek a deeper understanding of issues, circumstances, and conditions that assail society's members, regardless of where they live. For her, it was never enough to understand things only at the service or "giving" level. She knew that only a limited understanding was available at the surface level of human responses and that, as a consequence, only a limited and temporary response would be the result. Her knowledge of God assured her of the central place that the human heart played in moving people to very different places in their relationships with each other and, even more importantly, in their relationship with God.

Dr. Bethune always understood that changes in values and genuine transformation are only possible when the heart becomes fully engaged, and that it is the heart that opens and prepares the mind (head) to receive new knowledge, worldviews, and interpretations of truths different from knowledge, worldviews, and interpretations previously clung to. Dr. Bethune's work with world leaders was successful precisely because all of her interactions were informed by her understanding of the pivotal role the heart must play in getting leaders to really listen to what she had to say. She understood that, ultimately, the willingness of leaders to identify, prioritize, and wrestle with matters of social, cultural, and political import—issues that really mattered to the masses—was inextricably connected to whether, at the level of the heart, it mattered to them. By reaching the hearts of society's leaders, Dr. Bethune was able to open and prepare their minds to receive new knowledge, new worldviews, and new interpretations. By first reaching the heart, Dr. Bethune laid the important groundwork of engaging the intellect (head) in order to successfully shift paradigms and move these leaders to look beyond both race and gender.

Dr. Bethune lived and worked to democratize society through transformative models of education that few others understood. Hers was a life devoted to young people and to community empowerment. As a social justice advocate, community leader, educator, and political figure, she was clearly ahead of her time.

If the life and works of Mary McLeod Bethune could be characterized as a movement, it might well have been called the Bethune Movement. And while Bethune's life and work have never been characterized in this way, it is not a far-fetched proposition. Hers was a life of enormous depth and breath. She was a visionary. She lived according to a God-given calling with a purpose that was ordained by God and continuously fed by the Holy Spirit. Bethune's life and work was, in fact, a prototype of the Transformative Leadership Movement in America, and Bethune herself was the pre-eminent transformative leader. Through her life and work, we have learned the important lesson of how Caring Communities serve to anchor change.

Both the transformative leadership style of *visionary* leaders like Mary McLeod Bethune and the transactional leadership style of *managerial* leaders must be present within all organizations. Moreover, a reasonable and expected tension must also be present between them. Notwithstanding this important fact, the challenge for leaders and their organizations is to address the need to ensure that changes in the behaviors of their congregants, students, and employees translate into changes in their beliefs and values. Civil rights leaders and activists faced a similar challenge. Hard won laws granting and/or safe-guarding the rights of African Americans and other minority groups, while effective in changing behavior, had little effect on changing perspectives, values, or attitudes—and certainly no effect on changing hearts. An oft-quoted Martin Luther King Jr. expression of the era easily captures this concern, "Laws cannot make a man love me; but they can keep him from lynching me."

As a transformative leader and teacher, both Dr. Bethune's verbal and nonverbal behaviors had their roots in what was in her heart and mind. An honest search of both heart and mind was the litmus test she employed for empowering the disenfranchised citizens who were active in a participatory democracy. She was a voice crying out for black Americans, white Americans, and for all of humanity. She spoke with holy boldness for international students in the same committed way that she spoke out for low-income men and women and all marginalized people around the world. From the coastal towns of Haiti to the inland communities of the Bahamas, Dr. Bethune brought people together who, even as they were being drawn into interaction and cooperation, had little understanding of the significant racial division that was a part of her own reality.

The visit by the KKK

So in the spiritual world, when you see a giant, remember the road you must travel to come up to his [her] side is not along the sunny lane where wildflowers ever bloom; but a steep, rocky, narrow pathway where the blasts of hell will almost blow you off your feet; where the sharp rocks cut the flesh, where the projecting thorns scratch the brow, and the venomous beast hiss on every side.
—E.A. Kilbourne writing in *L. B.* Cowan's
Streams in the Desert

The day that Dr. Bethune learned that the local branch of the Ku Klux Klan was preparing to pay her a visit was similar to many others, and yet it would prove to be a day unlike any before or after. The daylight hours were nearly spent. As dusk approached, Dr. Bethune's unwavering faith in God steeled her as she told the members of her college family to "fear not." When dusk arrived, she instructed staff and students to dim the lights in the building. Coming onto the campus as a show of their displeasure with Bethune's efforts to register blacks to vote, the Klan was determined to confront her and anyone standing with her. She heard their footsteps, and exercising the very faith that brought her to Daytona from Palatka, Bethune began singing the words of the hymn, "God Will Take Care of You." Seconds later, the voices of the students and staff could he heard joining her in a harmonious chorus. Then something completely unexpected happened. As the singing grew louder and every word in each of the hymns sounded loudly and clearly, the Klansmen paused, then stopped their movement up the walkway toward the entrance to the college. Within only a few minutes of their arrival, they quietly turned around and left the campus grounds.

When Bethune was asked by the national media to comment on the Klan's abrupt departure, she explained that she was fairly certain that most, if not all, of the Klansmen were faithful churchgoers. Even more importantly, she added, the song that she, her students, and staff had sung was very likely familiar to them and may have been one that they themselves sang as members of their own congregations, reminding them of the very thing they witnessed in Dr. Bethune: faith in God. The words to the hymns proved powerful enough to gain access to the affective domain of learning. Dr. Bethune effectively touched the hearts of the Klansmen because they were immediately linked to their own congregations and the messages of the Gospel.

While not necessarily creating lasting mental or cognitive changes, it was obvious that something had touched the hearts of enough of the Klansmen to turn them away from their goal of terrorizing Bethune and those present at the school. If the Klan had been interviewed later, would we have discovered that many shifted their behavior based on an awakening of Christian consciousness just long enough to keep the campus safe? Bethune did get their attention, and while we might not understand every aspect of what happened, we do know that the Klan never returned to campus again.

The KKK obviously came to campus with something very different in mind—some ugly intention, goal, or course of action. And yet, its members did not carry out their original plans. Did the Klan change its mind about all blacks? Of course, they did not. But something did happen that night that interrupted their mission to terrorize, and it is this that begs for reflection and analysis.

Dr. Bethune's work and mission was that of building coalitions, empowering all citizens of the community, first with faith and then the knowledge that "greater is he that is in you then he that is in the world." By creating projects that were deliberately designed to bring her school and the community together as one large Caring Community, coalitions were formed and nourished. As a transformative leader, she was clearly a catalyst for reflection and a doorway leading to a genuine transition in values.

In spite of America's racial divide, Bethune spoke the language of identification (Burke 1950). She connected with others because, first and foremost, she saw all people as members of the human family, a family that had God at its head. She was extraordinarily good at bringing diverse people and groups together precisely because she believed in possibilities and, like me, perpetually asked, "Why not?" Hers was a message characterized by the presence of such qualities as mutual openness, nonmanipulativeness, recognition of uniqueness, unconditional positive regard, turning toward or presentness, and nonevaluation (Johannesen 1971). When she spoke, she touched hearts and opened doors of hope because hers was the language of the bridge builder who has made a commitment to closing the gap between human differences—gaps that pose enormous challenges between institutions of higher learning, churches, businesses, and the residents who live in their shadows.

The foundation for the Caring Community was laid through the life, work, and the legacy of Mary McLeod Bethune. Her love for humanity, her belief in the exceptional potential of each individual, and her resolve to use every available resource to build, uplift, and edify every man, woman, and child was always conscious and always deliberate. This is precisely what is called for today. The Caring Community will not just happen. It will not evolve on its own. Rather, for organizations in which such communities are absent, efforts to create the Caring Community must be conscious and deliberate. And whenever churches, schools, businesses, and other types of organizations are blessed to develop such communities, all stops must be pulled out to continuously nourish and sustain them. Dr. Bethune understood these things very well and so, too, must we. The onus for modeling Bethune's excellent example of the Caring Community falls on any and all who would call themselves leaders.

How can you love God whom you have never seen,
and hate your brother whom you see every day?

—1 John 4:20

Mary McLeod Bethune's legacy is fantastic in the countless ways in which she embraced the community and championed the concerns and causes of its men, women, and children. In her mind, she and the community were one. The community and the institution she founded were also one. For Bethune, this perspective needed to be extolled. Moreover, in Bethune's view, institutions of higher learning have a moral obligation to those communities that surround them. It is an obligation that goes beyond hiring men who women who happen to reside in the community. It goes beyond supporting various community agencies and organizations through the purchase of tickets for their respective events and fundraisers. It is an obligation to be an active member and participant of the community. It is the institution's obligation and commitment to stand and be counted as a trusted servant of the community.

In this first decade of the new millennium, the responsibility is on leaders (church, school, and business) to get it right—to embrace communities and their residents where they are. And, while town-grown tensions might exist, they must never be allowed to persist. I am reminded of an experience shared with me by a colleague. She told me of a community meeting she attended while waiting for the start of her first academic year as a professor. She was new to the institution and new to the community.

It was just a week or so prior to the start of the school year when, while reading the local newspaper, my colleague learned that a community meeting was scheduled for the local Police Athletic League (PAL). This meeting would bring residents and members of the Daytona Beach Police Department together to dialogue about police/citizen relations. Seeing her attendance as an excellent opportunity to also learn more about the community's relationship with the institution, she decided to attend the meeting. The faculty member viewed being new to the community a decided benefit, since she knew only a handful of people knew her.

The meeting was well attended, with residents voicing a variety of concerns about police department practices and the department's overall relationship with the African American community. Many of the residents suggested solutions and, in particular, identified sources of help and support from the larger community. To her chagrin, at no time during this ninety-minute meeting did any participant mention her new employer as a source of help or as a resource. Furthermore, not a single resident identified a professor, staff person, or student group that could be called upon at the institution for help. My colleague found this absence both extremely painful and very revealing. Like Dr. Bethune and me, my colleague felt very strongly that a central role of the academy (churches and businesses as well) is to make its presence felt within the lives of the men, women, children that surround the institution.

Certainly, our role is to become more proactive than reactive. As residents of public housing talked with passion and concern about their various interactions and encounters with the police department, through personal stories and storytelling, the affective domain of learning had been accessed. My colleague was moved. Her emotions were touched. Though a stranger to the community and its residents, she was not a stranger to the feelings and emotions their personal stories and experiences produced within her. She was far from a stranger from what her heart felt as she sat in on this meeting in August 1990.

It is clear that transformative learning must be understood as a process and not an event. It must be viewed through its various stages, with each stage being accompanied by clear guidelines and specific actions. While radical shifts in behavior and attitude might be possible, it is much more likely and far more desirable that the changes will be gradual, increasing the likelihood that they will be lasting rather than ephemeral. Change for the sake of change is not what transformational learning or leadership is about. Transformational learning and transformative leadership must be understood as processes that enable a consistent and critical evaluation of the ways in which we routinely view reality. In the absence of such an evaluation, it is impossible to produce the kind of leaders needed for our rapidly changing world.

Transformative leaders are needed in every leadership context, including business, the military, government sectors, the academy, and of course, our churches. The world around us is changing so rapidly that it is difficult to predict what the future holds. What we do know with certainty, to use an expression often heard among individuals who are a part of formal twelve-step recovery programs, is, "If you keep doing what you're doing, you'll just keep getting what you've got."

A truer statement could not be made about the critical importance of transformative learning, thinking, and those who would become transformative leaders. Taking just a few moments to reflect on the crises in leadership in events and situations from New Orleans to Myanmar, from Capitol Hill to Iraq, from country wide mortgage investments to oil giants like Exxon and Shell, inform us of just how true this is.

It is time that, as leaders, we become proactive in responding to the planet's crisis in leadership. However, our response must not be reminiscent of leadership models of the nineteenth and twentieth centuries because so many of those models reinforced and perpetuated the status quo. Rather, our response must be informed and guided by transformative learning and transformative leadership. Wide-awake leaders will commit, as an inherent duty and a moral obligation, to moving quickly into the twenty-first century, bringing those congregants, students, and employees who might go along with us. Our role must be to embrace emancipatory learning in order to develop leaders who are lifelong change agents precisely because they are lifelong learners, ready and capable of adapting to the needs of those they serve on the home front and the whole of society. It is said that you either plan to succeed or you plan to fail. Clearly, leaders and organizations who continue to function on maintenance mode are, in effect, planning their own demise because, without transformation, they will surely die.

We have seen the ways in which Mary McLeod Bethune used service learning as a way to access the spiritual domain of learning. We have seen how clearly she understood that the way to gain access to the minds of humanity was to gain access to their emotions—access to the hearts of men, women, and children. We now have a much more accurate understanding of what becomes possible when human beings are embraced with kindness and a genuine spirit of care and connectedness. It is now no secret that, if we really want to get the attention of the minds of men and women long enough to effect powerful change in America, we must first and foremost touch their hearts. Finally, it should be clear beyond qualification that, through service initiatives and volunteerism, mission outreach ministries represent an enormously powerful vehicle for accessing the spiritual domain of both pastors and the congregations they lead.

Dr. Mary McLeod Bethune first formed a Caring Community that led to individual and systemic change within Daytona Beach, Washington, D.C., and every place where she formed nurturing communities for dialogue, reflection, critique, and action.

But there is hope! If Dr. Mary McLeod Bethune transformed a nation toward acceptance, tolerance, and forgiveness, the church can surely lead a movement of congregational revitalization. This powerful story illustrates how Dr. Bethune activated the spiritual domain through her work and development of Caring Communities. She transformed a city, a nation, and the world. Her legacy is a reminder of the important role of the Caring Community.

Chapter IV

Leading Church Revitalization

○ ○ ○ ○ ○ ○ ○ ○ ○ ○ ○ ○ ○ ○ ○ ○ ○

And they that shall be of thee shall build the old waste places: thou shalt raise up the foundations of many generations; and thou shalt be called, The repairer of the breach, The restorer of paths to dwell in.

Isaiah 58:12

How does a servant of God begin to repair a breach? This is not asked to stump the reader. Rather this question should be seen as the light that moves slowly around the top of a lighthouse. Its movement is slow but ever so deliberate. It takes in all that might be seen within its range to prevent hurt, harm, and danger as it shines outward and as we shine it on ourselves as a community of Christians, especially as a community of Christian leaders. It is time to return to our belief in what we are told in Romans 8:28, "And we know that *all* things work together for good to them that **love** God, to them who are the called according to [his] purpose." All things work for the good for those who love the Lord. This includes an examination of our leadership as clergypeople and laity.

Addressing church revitalization, I thought about where we are today as a church family and as a church community. I reflected on what I have observed over the last few years as I have visited churches as a guest speaker and as a workshop presenter and facilitator. I've paid very close attention to what I've seen and even more attention to what I have not seen. I've been particularly interested in and concerned about the presence of those things that have had, and continue to have, a devastating effect on the Body of Christ as seen through shrinking congregations, irregular attendance, and a general sense by growing numbers of Christians that church homes that used to feed them don't any longer. And so it seemed to me that opening with Scripture that talked about repairing the breach was exactly the way to begin.

Webster's dictionary defines the term "breach" as an infraction or violation of a law, obligation, tie, or standard. It is also defined as a broken, ruptured, or torn condition. Additionally, it is defined as a temporary gap in continuity. This is precisely what I very strongly feel is our charge today. God is calling clergy and laity to repair the breach. He is calling us to get busy making repairs, making amends, mending fences, rebuilding relationships, reconnecting, re-establishing, and recommitting. He is calling us to do something different, if we are serious about getting different results. He is calling us to "be ye transformed," even as Paul was transformed on the road to Damascus. God wants us out of the box of traditional thinking ... thinking that refuses to create learning spaces where our hard-held assumptions can be reexamined, critiqued, adjusted, evolved, or removed. In clergy, God calls forth a new and different kind of leadership ... a "why not" and "what if" kind of leadership ... leadership that is truly visionary, that reflects the power of discernment, that refuses to be suffocated by traditions, that is compelling in its mission and, therefore, that produces the kind of results Christ knew were possible when he repeatedly admonished the disciples saying, "If you would only believe."

And so, we begin. We begin by first taking an honest look at where we are today as a direct consequence of trying to do God's work inside of a box.

It is safe to say that those churches that are growing have visionary pastors and laypeople who challenge their congregations to take a leap of faith. The members of these congregations are being challenged to reach outside the walls of the church and touch the very fabric of their communities (i.e., homeless, drug addicts, and displaced citizens; other cultures that do not have English as their first language; single parents; youth and young adults). The message is clear; it is not enough to invite these people into the church without first understanding and accepting them for who they are. Even more importantly, for what they have the potential to become! This is a tremendous challenge for congregations whose members are seniors. When the average age within a congregation is sixty-plus, change can be just too frightening, and sadly, some congregations would rather die in the present time as a congregation than become transformed for the future. Happily, there are congregations that understand and desire to change; however, even those with a sincere desire to change are inhibited from doing so for a variety of reasons.

I was called in to facilitate an inner city congregation that was on life support. Every member declared that the church was dead. They confessed to wanting change to occur and invited me in to lead and facilitate a workshop. The average age of the membership of this particular congregation was seventy. We identified a variety of challenges, including the location, which was in a downtown area where the population had dwindled and most residents had relocated to the suburbs. After the participants identified the reasons why the church was failing, we turned our attention to what we wanted the church to become and the types of ministries it needed. The focus was then on refining the mission statement for this local congregation.

Perhaps because I was the facilitator, I felt very good about the progress the laypeople and clergy were making because they were being honest and forthcoming about their status and desire to change. After a full day of praying, reflecting, and planning, one outcome of this session was a desire to change the music program. When I inquired what they had in mind, all of the senior citizens observed that they liked and enjoyed singing hymns but wanted to bring gospel and more lively music into play to attract younger members. I posed many questions to this team and left feeling rewarded and hopeful.

Some months later, I attended this church and wondered why the same music program was still in place. During that same Sunday, a young male visitor appeared in blue jeans and looked out of place in the barely filled church as the regular members were dressed in their Sunday best suits and clothing. When visitors were acknowledged and asked to stand and give his or her name and church home, this young man stated: *"I am here to find Jesus. I have lost my way in life and just wanted to visit."* My heart was warmly touched even as I observed that many people visiting our churches may not have church homes. I have often wondered how they feel when they must fit into our traditions and assumptions. Nevertheless, the service ended and I peered to the back door to observe this young man walking slowly out the church without a single person engaging him in conversation or welcoming him to the place where he wanted to find Jesus. It appeared that I was literally leaping over the pews to touch him and to state: "You have come to the right place." I recalled immediately taking him downstairs to the fellowship hall and personally introducing him to the pastor and several ushers who had a lot of power and influence in this congregation. After engaging in a short conversation, we discovered that this young man was a musician who had dropped out of church and society because of drug use and abuse.

I wish I could tell you this story has a happy ending for both the church and the young man. It does not. In spite of what these congregants said they wanted, not a single member of this church bothered to contact the young man. I inquired through several telephone calls to the visitor and was not only shocked but hurt by the lack of investment in the human soul by a congregation that not only claimed to save souls but dared to declare they wanted to grow and to revitalize their church.

This church had a leader who wanted to change but did not have vision. In the end, the entire team of clergy and laity only wanted to feel safe in tradition. They invited me in for their retreat because they desired vision, but they could not claim it.

Recently, my spouse volunteered to create a beautiful flower garden in the entrance of the local church. However, one member was deeply hurt when a plant was removed that had special meaning through a memorial gift. My husband and I reflected on whether the plant should have been removed without notice to church leaders, and while we certainly did not mean to hurt a fellow parishioner's feelings or sensibilities, we quickly reached the conclusion that until our faith walk is consumed with the Great Commission—the work of saving souls as opposed to saving traditions—we might as well close the doors to our churches. Our focus must be on finding out why so many of our young people are in prison instead of in our churches. When the energy of clergy and laity is drained because of an unwillingness to set aside traditional ways of thinking and move beyond assumptions, laboring in the vineyard will continue to be a lonely charge. Diversions to our charge and mission are, in fact, diversions to God's work. Even as we think about the need to overcome traditional barriers to thinking in order to retain and draw new members to mainstream churches, the need to focus our attention on the price of not having a compelling mission cannot be overstated.

Church revitalization is possible if and when congregational leaders understand the power and potential within this continuous learning process of transformative leadership. Revitalization must involve building Caring Communities, feeding the spiritual dimension of members, and modeling inviting behaviors.

Activating the Spiritual Domain

Throughout our discussion of the roles of Caring Communities and the process of transformative leadership, I have talked about the importance of activating the spiritual domain. And while there are many lenses into the spiritual dimension of leadership, several are discussed below:

(1) Service Learning and Mission Outreach

> *What am I to do? I expect to pass through this world but once. Any good work, therefore, any kindness, or any service I can render to any soul of man [person] or animal, let me do it now. Let me not neglect or defer it, for I shall not pass this way again.*
> —Old Quaker Saying

As previously stated, one lens into the spiritual domain is mission outreach programs and service learning projects, which also foster Caring Communities. As different individuals work together on projects that bring them new insights, their hearts are touched and Caring Communities are built.

I remember a very conservative gentleman, who I will refer to as Wayne. I worked with Wayne in my early career with the church. He was known for his very static thinking and views about others. He was quite judgmental, and I was sure that he had little interest in really getting to know me or my journey. Many of us declared that Wayne would prove hopeless in any effort to accept those who were different from him because he was one of millions of average white-collar male workers of that time period.

Along the way, Wayne traveled to Africa on a mission trip. Once there, he observed poverty and hunger unlike anything he had ever seen. Firsthand, he saw sick people going without treatment because they simply had no medicine. Wayne saw suffering and hopelessness. As a result of this mission trip, he became a transformed person; Wayne was forever changed. His heart had been opened, and whether he wanted to or not, he would never be able to return to his prior self.

Just as Wayne had been transformed and, thereby, moved to new paradigms and new ways of seeing the world and the different realities of its various peoples, local congregations can also become transformed. They can become revitalized and become vital communities. Churches can become the change they want to see.

Within university settings and corporate entities, service learning is becoming a part of the organizational mission because of intrinsic and extrinsic gain. I am always interested in learning about my colleagues' experiences as they teach their classes, meet with their students, or become excited about their research or a manuscript that has been accepted by a refereed journal in their field. I am especially excited when I have the opportunity to hear from a faculty or staff person about an outreach or service learning experience. Such was the case recently, when a faculty member at my university shared with me how her involvement in service learning led her to a transformational encounter with the Holy Spirit.

Before I took over the helm of the university where I now serve as president, the institution received a Ford Foundation grant to institutionalize service learning. The year was 1994 and Bethune-Cookman was one of ten historically black colleges whose charge was to infuse service learning into the curriculum. The university-wide program was known as Project Reclaim and began with every single student devoting a minimum of fifteen hours to off-campus civic engagement during the second semester of their freshman year.

The faculty member shared with me that over the course of the life of Project Reclaim, tremendous accomplishments were made, especially in closing the gap between "town and gown." English and business majors tutored and mentored children in after-school programs, with as many as three hundred students giving hours to the local Police Athletic League during the course of a single week. Students from all majors read to pre-K boys and girls enrolled in Head Start programs. Students who majored in criminal justice and psychology joined teenage males and females as positive role models in sessions conducted by employees of the Department of Juvenile Justice.

Students majoring in disciplines within the social sciences worked with families trying to get back on their feet through various family renew efforts. Those who majored in the sciences put on science and math teach-ins. All across the disciplines, students showed up on Saturdays to provide extra tutoring for children whose school attendance was uncertain because of health crises associated with having sickle cell anemia. Students put the finishing touches on homes that were renovated for low-income residents through the local community development corporation. They painted the homes of senior citizens who qualified for the city's house painting program but were unable to take advantage of it because they had no one to do the painting. Music majors formed community choirs and students, offering their gifts as dance instructors and choreographers for community youth. The theme song for the program was "Lean on Me."

Service learning energy was high, and after a couple of years, the university was asked to host the annual conference of the Ford/UNCF Community Service Partnership Project (CSPP). Planning had been fierce and the campus was abuzz with talk about the upcoming conference because faculty, staff, and administrators had observed the transformation in students, in the community, and in the institution's relationship with its neighbors. The professor who was the director of the program went on to tell me that as she drove over to the beach on the evening of the opening reception, the Holy Spirit spoke to her so powerfully that she was forced to drive her vehicle onto a service station lot and just stop. She shared with me that the words were crystal clear and that she hears them today just as clearly as she heard them fourteen years ago: "This is God's work and he is well pleased." She cried and knew with an unshakeable certainty that the institution's and her own calling was precisely in doing what they were being blessed to do.

I am in full agreement with my professor: service learning is God's work. Indeed, service learning and mission are uniquely intertwined. How better to connect with the people of God than through the up close and personal experiences that service learning creates? It is difficult to put into words the "holy moments" made possible through service learning. These moments are so pleasing in God's sight. Far too many people miss the extraordinary power inherent in opportunities for students, workers, and congregants to experience life and their faith as service learners.

There are those who think of service learning as volunteerism. There are others who characterize service learning as an "us helping them or those people" obligation. Nothing could be further from the truth. The truth is that when we engage in authentic service learning, we feed our own spirits. Service learning is an exceptional vehicle for opening the affective domain, causing human beings to see others as they see themselves— causing human beings to find far more similarities than differences in each other. It's moving human beings very effectively to the place where they can honestly speak the African saying, "I am because you are."

Service learning is so much more than "giving back." When the senior citizen in the wheel chair says, "I thought nobody cared," the affective domain has been opened and we are changed. When the six-year-old who is just beginning to read looks up into your face after having sounded a word that was initially a struggle, you can always see into her soul, if ever so briefly. The spiritual domain has been opened, and we are transformed. When in a group setting, a young woman confesses that she hates Father's Day and then tells the group why, the spiritual domain has been opened and we are transformed.

Churches are called to aggressively seek the unsaved through service learning. We are called to get up close and ever so personal to those we might lead to Christ. We are called to leap over church pews to invite, embrace, and encourage those who come, and leave the confines of the church building for those who have not. Mission carried out through service learning means meeting people where they are. It means showing up and allowing ourselves to be used. It is absent of prejudging and judging. It seeks the homeless and the abused, as well as the abuser. Through service learning, we allow ourselves to be used in ways that are the most meaningful to those who call on us and those we encounter.

Dr. Bethune understood service learning well. And even though the term was not used during her lifetime, the truth of its relevance and importance found itself within her essence as a leader, as a citizen of the world, and as a lover of humanity. She understood the power of embracing a spirit of reciprocity and avoided the nearly fatal mistake of approaching others as their "saviors" or rescuers. She knew from her own life's work the enormous lessons to be taught by and learned from ordinary people, just as I recognized and embraced the wealth of knowledge and the wisdom the elders of my Caring Community imparted to me and the other children of my youth.

Respect for service learning and mission outreach are really about respect for God's purpose and the gifts that God had deposited in each of us. A desire to embrace service learning reflects wisdom and a genuine understanding of what God has called us to do both for and with each other. Writing in *Streams in the Desert*, author Adelaide Proctor says,

> It isn't the thing you do, dear
> It's the thing you leave undone,
> Which gives you the bitter heartache
> At the setting of the sun;
> The tender word unspoken,
> The letter you did not write,
> The flower you might have sent, dear
> Are your haunting ghosts at night.
>
> The stone you might have lifted
> Out of your brother's way,
> The bit of heart some counsel
> You were hurried too much to say;
> The living touch of the hand, dear,
> The gentle and winsome tone,
> That you had no time or thought for;
> With troubles enough of your own.
>
> These little acts of kindness,
> So easily out of mind,
> These chances to be angels,
> Which even mortals find.
>
> They come in night and silence,
> Each chill reproachful wraith,
> When hope is faint and flagging,
> And a blight has dropped on faith.

For life is all too short, dear.
And sorrow is all too great,
To suffer our slow compassion
That tarries until too late.
And it's not the thing you do, dear,
It's the thing you leave undone,
Which gives you the bitter heartache,
At the setting of the sun.

As one lens into the spiritual domain, service learning is also quite powerful in addressing the "isms" of our time period.

(2) "Call" to a Compelling Mission

A strong call to a compelling mission is another lens into the spiritual domain. This call is owned and valued by every member in the organization, and many people describe this call as similar to the call experienced by clergy who enter the ministry. It is a mistake to conclude that our mission statements are what touches the hearts of others. Rather, it is the purpose behind a mission that is linked to our ability to influence positive change that will make a difference and leave a lasting legacy. For example, if we are called to respond to world hunger and we have a specific way of making a difference, we have, in fact, been blessed with a lens into the spiritual domain that has the power to change our lives forever. Vital congregations have a mission that is embraced by their members with passion, commitment, and faith. Once we see dying children firsthand, we are compelled to work and give in order to eliminate this cause of such pain and suffering. We become deeply touched by seeing the difference we are able to make as we respond to the problem of world hunger through a village program or aimed at a particular family in a developing country.

It is difficult to have a vital congregation when its leader does not know where it is headed or where it desires to be. So many churches are operating on tradition rather than revisiting their mission goals. For congregations that do not have a mission beyond their weekly worship service and occasional program events, I wish to pose the following questions:

"Where does God want our church to be?"
"How do we get there?"
"Who needs to be involved?"
"Who are the recipients of our outreach, including our own
congregation and its members?"
"What groups are we leaving out?"
"Have we been in the trenches with those we desire to serve?"
"How might we become transformed to do God's work?"
"How can we all participate?"
"What is our image externally?"
"How do we discern where God is leading us?"

It is through prayer, reflection, and effective facilitation that pastors and members begin to respond honestly and freely to these questions. These questions are also lenses for accessing the spiritual domain.

While these spiritual lenses are necessary for our growth and wisdom-seeking, there are persistent forces that impede their use. Resistance and complaints about taking time to activate this domain of learning and discerning should come as no surprise. Indeed, they are more common than I would like to think. However, to become vital, we must first recognize that our vision needs correction. Just as we purchase eyeglasses because we want to see as clearly and as accurately as possible, the church must understand that it is through its vitality and clearer vision that it will reach urban communities and the world's hurting men, women, and children.

Vital congregations are led by the Holy Spirit in a process that is intended to be transformational and to transform the world. This process is often aborted by those who do not want to embrace needed change for kingdom building. For this process to work, all participants must enter into covenant to pose the hard questions and be open for the faith walk. I will often share with Caring Community participants that this process creates dis-ease and discomfort because it is difficult for many congregations to make even the slightest movement in a different direction. A facilitator is useful to create a neutral ground swell of dialogue. Prayer is essential!

(3) Building Covenant Groups

It is through prayer, daily devotion, Bible studies, and community sharing that Caring Communities enter a covenant and hold one another accountable. The ritual of entering into covenant can be a lens into the spiritual domain. Forming a spiritual partnership through ritual can also be extremely powerful and very emotional. Outside consultants are often useful in this process to raise questions and to seek directions that will be owned by the community of faith. I have seen at least a dozen churches become vital as a result of a covenant process that moves the participants from their logical processes of reasoning toward their hearts.

I have personal experience with entering a covenant as I participated in such a process in my early years as a member of an dying inner city congregation. We brought in an outside consultant who questioned us about who we wanted to become. We shared our dreams and visions. We committed our time to six intensive working and discerning sessions. Each member bonded with others as we ended up revitalizing our church membership with innovation, productive community outreach, and dramatic transition in our ability to make miracles happen. Our church giving increased, our Sunday School classes grew, and our worship hour became a wonderful expression of God's grace. We concluded our process by executing a covenantal agreement that guided us toward success.

(4) Storytelling

Storytelling has a somewhat similar emotional impact on people as testimonials. While most testimonials relate to the individual's disclosure of God's action in his/her life, storytelling can move peoples' emotions through illustrations about self and others. These stories can be most powerful in awakening the spiritual dimension. The act of telling the story and/or hearing the other's story is the lens that most of my study participants cited as facilitating their dramatic transformation in both values and beliefs.

In a group exercise, a facilitator shared the following story. It was a powerful tool for fostering both dialogue and reflection:

A homeless person named Grace was a middle-aged woman who had recently lost her job. She lived in her car and felt broken. She was so ashamed and very depressed. Grace explained that, at first, she was so immobilized that she did not seek help. She confessed that the last place she wanted to go was to church. First, she was not presentable, and secondly, she felt like a failure. Lastly, Grace said that she felt that God had abandoned her, and then she went on to describe what it felt like to exist in a world where people did not care about her. A stranger saw Grace on the street and stated: "We are all one paycheck away from being homeless. How can our church make a difference?"

Intervention by facilitator: After sharing Grace's story, the facilitator asked the congregation, "What can, or should, we do with people like Grace?" After much discussion and reflection about how Grace's story could become a reality for any of them and/or their family members, that congregation decided to start an outreach program for the homeless. Before very long, more people joined the congregation and word spread about a vital ministry that valued community caretaking. A number of homeless people were helped to find gainful employment, and many became active in the church's ministries.

Reflection: Grace is the face of so many unchurched people who feel uninvited into our congregations. The dress codes, the sterile stares, and even the anguished feeling that results from being "put on the spot" when asked to stand and give their names and church affiliations. This can be a terrifying experience, one which keeps the unchurched from coming or from returning. Grace candidly shared with us that, while this congregation thought it was placing a welcome sign out front, she felt very uninvited.

I really listened to the story about Grace, and I learned more than I could ever articulate within these pages. Because we genuinely listened, we all learned a lot that day. The transformation that was needed for a new and revised church mission was created because our hearts were touched by a story that connected us to another human being.

The local church is perhaps the largest educator of adults and children in the world. Through mission and ministry, pastors and laity have the ability to convey both knowledge and values. Furthermore, churches transform lives and the world through outreach and mission. The church should be known as a place that models transformative leadership and role modeling toward the building and restoring of Caring Communities.

(5) Shared Leadership That Is Grounded in Ethics

One of the mistakes congregations make is to place the mantle of leadership squarely on the shoulders of their pastors. Within the concept of Caring Communities, all members of the congregation assume responsibility and roles associated with leadership. The act of empowering those who do not think of themselves as leaders is another lens that activates the heart. Nothing seems to move others more than to see a value, ability, gift, or strength that they have yet to see in themselves.

Shared participation and respect for the gifts of others always touches hearts. Respect for the individual gifts of group members is even more meaningful when the community operates within ethical principles. Elements of "fairness" and "goodness" enhance our connection to Scripture as we live out our faith in community. Every person desires to offer his/her gifts, just as they also desire their contributions to be valued. And while this is certainly true, it is important to be vigilant about separating one's desire to offer gifts for building God's kingdom from any and all negative uses of power intended for self-gain or the reinforcement of egocentric behavior. Effective leadership is about empowerment, mutuality, and valuing diversity in the talents and gifts of others.

> Leadership is dynamic, evolutionary, and fundamentally a part of life that cannot be relegated to a position, role, individual, or a set of characteristics. Because leadership is as complex as life itself, the process of learning to lead must engage the whole person in community through mental, physical, spiritual, and eschatological components of the human psyche linked to others to facilitate critique and reflective practice. (Reed, 1993)

Because effective leadership is causative, acts of change must reflect both behavioral and internal transition whereby the leader and "followers" undergo internal reviews of their assumptions and habitual ways of thinking.

Effective leadership must always be grounded in ethical principles of humanistic goals and also be understood as a continuous process of learning to lead. Caring Communities should be ethical communities that formulate multiple directions, all leading to kingdom building. As the ethically centered Caring Community explores new possibilities, it moves toward a planning process in which all participants share equally in the discussion of strategic change. Moreover, as all participants share equally in decision-making, dialogue, and acts of a Caring Community, an opening of the spiritual domain becomes the motivator for reflection and the critique of one's assumptions and habitual ways of judging and perceiving reality.

It is not unusual for transformative partners/collaborators of visionaries to express uncertainty about their roles and responses to innovations. The Caring Community concept does not rely on a pecking order of leaders because each participant is empowered fully in the process of dialogue and group reflection. Leaders and followers must communicate doubts and uncertainties as soon as possible, without appearing to be reactionary. Leaders must understand their partners/collaborators by listening and sharing fully in the participation and support of these communities. As a visionary leader, I will never forget my complete shock when a key member of my leadership team stated simply, "I don't understand what you are doing."

This was just after I had worked hard to raise $8 million to build a new science building on another campus where I served as president/CEO. While it was perfectly clear to me that I was waiting to build the infrastructure of the organization, this member of my leadership team reacted only to the pressure that he felt to change from maintenance-oriented management to a higher level of accountability. My initial reaction to his question was to conclude that he was not supportive of my leadership. However, upon deeper reflection, I concluded that I was guilty of failing to accomplish each of the important processes of empowerment. It is important that the transformative leader knows that his/her partners/collaborators see value in him or her being at the helm and that they have every intention of being supportive. It is also important that partners/collaborators admit the need to get a better understanding of the vision and the direction, whenever it is apparent that styles differ. Partners/collaborators should ask for clarification on innovations and changes and then openly express any apprehension and fears that are the result of embarking on the new journey with a new leader. Within group dialogue sessions, leadership challenges may be framed for debate and clarification.

Transformative leaders must understand that change may threaten others, especially whenever stakeholders have not embraced the changes as their own or fail to understand the goals of the innovation or change. Members of the leadership team must be willing to help the transformative leader appreciate that change frightens those who have not had time to understand the change, the change agent, or the change process.

When I assumed my first presidency, I was totally unprepared for negative responses to successful fundraising, but this is exactly what confronted me. Fundraising at the first institution I led as president was remarkable in its limitations. After 122 years, a total of $3 million had been raised. Through transformative leadership methods, we were able to raise $30.5 million in two and a half years. Erroneously, I assumed that the stakeholders would be ecstatic. They were not. Instead, as soon as the first new facility went up, a state-of-the-art library/technology building, campus conversations centered on the transformative leader instead of the transformation. Though questions like, "Who does she think she is?" and "Why is she moving so quickly?" served no useful purpose, they nonetheless moved quickly throughout the institution.

What I had not taken into consideration was that some stakeholders felt exposed and insecure because what they had not accomplished during their tenure was now being done. This was especially true for key members of the leadership team, who had been with the institution or in certain positions for many years. Mistakenly, others felt they could not share in the credit for the dramatic changes they were seeing. They felt left behind when my intention was to build new paradigms that would remain long after my tenure at the institution. Some people were even envious that I, a woman president, the first in that institution's history, had managed to gain support in a much wider range of places and with donors who had not previously supported the small African American liberal arts institution that I had led. According to some mindsets, the transformative leader was an "outsider" and had not paid her dues in that community.

The mistake I made was clear: I had not effectively built support for the change by involving the surrounding community and all stakeholders in the vision. While the trustees and major alumni were engaged in the fundraising process, the community at large did not understand the process for change, nor did I offer them an opportunity to share in the credit for the visionary changes.

Much too often, transformative leaders assume that the charge they lead will translate into excitement among those they view as their partners and collaborators. This is a serious mistake! Stakeholders must feel a part of the change, or at least understand what is taking place. Without deliberate efforts to bring the community on board at the outset, transformative leaders run the risk of alienating those who might otherwise have been among their strongest advocates. We must also give public and sincere credit for the changes to our various constituencies. Without them, there would be little success.

Having learned from this experience, my next presidency was characterized by both conscious and deliberate efforts to advocate change through shared vision ownership with partners/collaborators (i.e., congregants, employees, students, etc.). This time, a deliberate investment of time was made to identify and build a collective new direction and seek joint ownership for a new vision. The result was affirmation from alumni, other stakeholders, and a growing acceptance from the community. This time, stakeholders and transformative partners/collaborators were continuously sharing in the credit for the institution's new direction.

Transformative leaders are like music conductors. While it is the conductor's role to direct the men, women, or children who constitute the choir or chorus, it is actually the choral group that produces the harmony and the sound. They actually make things happen!

Many years ago, Mahatma Gandhi said that we should be the change that we hope to see. The change that we must, in fact, see in the church community has its roots in transformative leaders who are pastors and laity who give of their various gifts of the spirit and more. If the world is to truly become all that Christ meant it to be "on Earth as it is in Heaven," then our charge is clear. Jesus said it best when he asked, "How can you love me whom you have never seen and hate my brother [sister] whom you see every day?"

When we fail to put the needs of our brothers and sisters first, then as men and women of God we have shown them that we hate them. When we fail to wait on the Holy Spirit and allow him to have his way because we've given in to pressure from church leaders to "be out by 1:00 and certainly no later than 1:30," we have shown them that we hate them. When we design ministries that operate at times that are convenient for us and open church offices like banks, from ten to two and never on the weekend or holidays, we have shown a lack of priority for mission and ministry. When we fight against those who bring innovation and change, those who see the benefits of thinking outside of the box, those who compel us to examine our firmly held assumptions, we have shown that we dishonor our Christian faith. We have blocked the will of God in our lives and theirs and have sorely grieved the Holy Spirit with whom we thirst to commune. In this respect, the contribution of the Caring Community is the act of engaging in dialogue to remove past assumptions, to prod for answers, to critique leadership, and to equally participate in framing new realities.

(6) Beyond Rituals and Ceremonies

The age-old statement from churches is, "We have always done it this way." Such a statement is characteristic of how the status quo is never challenged, let alone examined. For these organizations to change, the spiritual domain is paramount.

Too many of our churches are in this type of holding pattern. Sadly, it seems they would rather die than change. Change is painful unless we are led by God and able to release our control over others to receive the gifts of the spirit. Although change is never easy, we know when it arrives, because our hearts are warmed and there is usually an inner peace that is found radiating in our soul. Transformative leadership is not a replacement for ministry. Rather, it is a catalytic agent for effective work that occurs inside and outside of the congregation, as well as through external outreach services. It has enormous potential for changing those who are most resistant to change.

What is most effective in planning and implementing ceremonies or rituals designed to release and let go of the past? Rituals perform well in opening the lens into the hearts of observers and participants. Many Caring Communities are deliberate in their efforts to create services and experiences that allow them to embrace change even as they continue to show a respect for the past. I witnessed a powerful covenant service where litanies and candles were used for a mutual commitment to service. Commissioning services and consecration ceremonies can also serve the same purpose of moving mindsets to an emotional realm for reflection and movement of the Spirit.

(7) Employing the Strategic Planning Process

Although strategic planning is thought of as a traditional process, it really has the capacity to engage visioning and innovative thinking. Once Caring Communities are formed and bonded, the leader or facilitator must encourage dreaming and visioning without restrictions and barriers. People must be granted permission to explore new and exciting changes. Then the leader must invite the community to create a plan of action to manifest their dreams. By inviting storytelling, testimonials, ideas, and music into a venue, visioning can take shape and support change within organizations. The creative aspect of dreaming is yet another lens into the domain of the spirit. Many of us have not been granted permission to dream and vision since we were children. Needless to say, proper facilitation is critical in order to engage visioning and innovative thinking in the traditional strategic planning process.

What is strategic change?

Strategic change is continuous reinvention of an organization's mission through innovation and shifts in services and outcomes in order to meet the needs of a rapidly changing, information-driven, and global society. Change that is strategic is derived from a continuously thoughtful and deliberate review of an institution's mission. The singular objective is to employ new inventions, diversity, and new opportunities that will enhance the institution's mission, thereby ensuring continued positive growth and institution-wide quality.

How can transformative leaders manage change when it is perceived that they are disrupting the organization's stability?

Concerns about how transformative leaders can usher in the changes they champion without being perceived as disrupting the stability of the organization (i.e., church, school, business) are justified. This is an extremely important question, especially for the transformative leader who is new to an organizational setting. It is important that clergypeople, leaders, and students view and appreciate change as layered sequentially from three organic levels.

The first level involves forming and bonding. The second level is the covenantal, where ground rules are set for the group related to participatory involvement, ethical frameworks, and group accountability. The third level involves the core action of transformative leadership related to framing issues for discussion, critique, reflection and, hopefully, discernment. Whenever a new member enters the group, they must start at the beginning. Jumping to the second or third level prohibits bonding, which is the prerequisite for movement toward an effective Caring Community. This is the reason the word "organic" is used to support the language of levels or stages. This process is not hierarchical. Rather, it is cyclical. Each level of the process must be given adequate consideration and attention if the proposed change and eventual implementation are to go smoothly.

What are essential questions to be posed of our constituents for Caring Communities?

- We need to know their stories, both personal and professional
- We need to know what is in both their hearts and minds
- We need to know their dreams for a better world
- We need to know how they enter into relationship with God

The first level of the transition is critical to the eventual success of subsequent stages inasmuch as it provides an important opportunity to bond and build trust.

The second level involves a marriage between participants where each understands roles and expectations for participating in Caring Communities. An actual articulation or covenant agreement should be signed by all participants. This will include some form of ceremony or ritual.

The third level launches the process of inquiry, critique, and reflection. Below are some questions that may initiate the dialogue.

General questions to ask stakeholders:

- ☐ How do you perceive our organization (church, school, business)?
- ☐ How do you think people outside of our organization perceive us?
- ☐ What gaps in our mission do you believe need to be filled?
- ☐ What are some of your own unmet needs?
- ☐ What do you think are some of the unmet needs of other members of our organization (church, school, business)?
- ☐ To what extent have your expectations of our organization (church, school, business) been met?
- ☐ Is the organization a caring and nurturing community?
- ☐ Within this environment, what are your dreams and aspirations?
- ☐ What are some of the barriers to spiritual, personal, and professional growth that you believe must be overcome?
- ☐ What role might you personally play in order to become more empowered and more actualized?
- ☐ In what ways have you been able to contribute to the organization?
- ☐ Do you sense you are in a Caring Community?

As a transformative leader, ask yourself the following questions:

- ☐ How can my relationship with all constituent groups (congregants, school stakeholders, workplace stakeholders, business environment stakeholders) be improved?
- ☐ Is the organization (church, school, business) I lead characterized by effective communication?
- ☐ Within the organization, what is working effectively?
- ☐ Where is change needed?
- ☐ Are you experiencing a Caring Community?

Transformative leaders need to be especially thoughtful when it comes to those individuals who will be invited to join them as policymakers. The goal is to form a Caring Community to support necessary and needed change. Whether a presidential cabinet member, a company's management or supervisory team member, a body of deacons and deaconesses, or a member of the student government, individuals who make up these bodies are enormously important to the transformative leader's ultimate success.

Transformative Leaders must work to ensure open responses from their primary support people on each of the following questions:

- ☐ Do they own the mission and vision of the organization?
- ☐ In what ways do they contribute to the organization?
- ☐ Are they clear on the distinction between policy and administration?
- ☐ Do they share in decision-making?
- ☐ Are they properly and thoroughly provided with resources to inform decision-making?
- ☐ Are they aware of and interested in the feedback received from constituents?
- ☐ Do they value a role which includes nurturing their team members to want a higher level of achievement and Caring Community?

Transformative leaders are uniquely focused on the recipients of services offered by the organization (i.e., church, business, student leadership group, employees, etc.). Subsequently, they ask a variety of extremely important questions.

Ideally, the following questions are posed to constituents regularly and, it is hoped, seldom in response to a failure or shortcoming of the church, business, or student leadership.

- ☐ Is the organization providing quality services?
- ☐ Are there gaps in service or services that are being provided by the organization?
- ☐ Would you say that the organization has failed in any particular leadership or response area?
- ☐ In your view, is the mission of the organization on target with the constituents it seeks to serve? If not, what suggestions do you have?
- ☐ Do you receive useful communication about the organization?
- ☐ Are there any innovations within the organization that you are especially pleased with?

☐ Do you think the organization has become stagnant?

☐ Does the organization feel like a family?

At the end of this book is a section with suggested exercises for building and sustaining Caring Communities.

The church, business, or student government body seeking responses to these and other important questions may select a variety of methods to gather information. These methods might range from town hall meetings to focus groups and, of course, surveys, which often are less threatening to those who want to share constructive feedback.

The principal responsibility of the transformative leader at this stage is to facilitate discussion, solicit input, and conduct a real-time analysis of all input. Each constituency group is provided with a final overview of the analysis, with special attention being given to the ways in which the data can be used to inform decisions. Additionally, the analysis should focus on any new insights gleaned from the data.

Having accomplished the above, the organization (i.e., church, school, business) is now adequately prepared to embark on a course of strategic planning and visioning. The leader has sought input and shared with his or her various constituencies the analysis derived from data. While only the leaders and/or policymakers will make the final decisions relative to change and innovation, most constituents are much more inclined to support any subsequent innovation or recommendation for change because they see themselves as having actively participated in the process leading to change. For the transformative leader, the goal is to make sure that all stakeholders are heard, valued, and taken seriously.

If there is one admonition at this point, it is that the leader must now involve key stakeholders in planning and must continue to make use of the participatory process.

How has transformative leadership impacted the strategic planning process?

The traditional view of the strategic planning process is one in which broad goals are established. The process has traditionally been described with the setting of goals that are consistent with and, indeed, reflect the organization's (church, school, business) mission statement and specific objectives. Timelines and benchmarks are created with the specific objectives in mind. Because the objectives are the action steps used to guide the organization toward the implementation of its specific goals, it is imperative that every sector within the organization participate in the process to ensure that results will be effectively coordinated. It should be noted that the greater the specificity of each objective, the easier their effectiveness can be evaluated.

Adherence to the timelines assigned to each specific objective is also viewed as a gauge of the organization's effectiveness.

To infuse elements of transformative leadership, a group will begin on a journey of discovery regarding where God is leading the organization. Each person will share not only a desire or expressed need, but the organization as a whole will move outwardly to first listen to every participant and compare reflections with Scripture.

Strategic planning in this respect is very suitable for groups beyond the church. I have successfully facilitated many organizational retreats on strategic planning where smaller break-out groups ended up with similar reports, moving the organization in a unified direction for a new strategic plan.

How is accountability viewed by the transformative leader?

It is additionally important that facilitators set aside time to describe to other participants precisely how the organization will implement accountability measures as a way to demonstrate the organization's overall effectiveness. Finally, effective communication and the impact of shared information within the group must never be underestimated! The implication of this point is that individual members should pair outside of group time to continue dialogue that started as a part of the transformative process.

So, Where Do We Go from Here?

Central to my personal philosophy of leadership is an uncompromising stance that it must be rooted in ethical principles and humanistic values. Therefore, any effort to design and develop curricula for church denominations, the academy, or business and industry must be soundly grounded in both. In my view, if a leadership curriculum is to be truly transformative and, therefore, effective, these elements must assume a central position. Caring Communities, in essence, represent a collective form of leadership. Just as the individual transformative leader has an important role to play in every organization so, too, do these communities. Both the Caring Community and the individual transformative leader strive for excellence in leadership and decision-making.

Effective leadership calls for an embrace of a new understanding of leader transformation. This new understanding assumes a commitment to engaging in a genuine analysis of leader-held assumptions in order to begin exploring new realities of one's world in "out of the box" ways. If leadership is to be effective, it must also rely on a critical *pedagogy* that fosters innovation and change within our global and rapidly changing society.

The process of transformation envisages the change of the social order against the ethical horizon of a fully realized (but not yet achieved) civic culture ... a culture that promotes the autonomy of all citizens as they work to build and engage in a participatory democracy. In Chapter I, the account of Jim's transformation saw him moving away from his previously held assumptions about the roles and "place" of women within the Methodist Church into a place where he was able to appreciate, value, and embrace the inclusion of women in more prominent positions within that denomination. Because of Jim's transformation, we must know that we, along with our congregations and organizations, are just as capable of change.

Forming Caring Communities: "Behold, I make all things new"

Just as the educational process is never neutral, nor are Caring Communities. How Caring Communities are formed is a topic whose value is incalculable. Many Caring Communities are launched through the use of outside facilitators who are invited in to organize and set up the necessary processes. It is extraordinarily important that these people remain vigilant about avoiding injecting their own biases, desires, and agendas into the environment. This is perhaps even more important whenever the facilitator is the pastor or other recognized authority within the church, school, or business. A similar admonition is extended to the laity or individual members of newly formed or existing communities.

They must be cautious about dominating discussions and attempting to force their own ideas and opinions onto other members of the community. Caring Communities are not intended to become therapy group sessions. Occasionally, communities will discover that within them are a few individuals who attempt to have their individual problems and challenges addressed through Caring Community sessions. Caring Communities are charged with developing ways to provide these individuals with positive feedback while at the same time making sure the dialogue process is not contaminated. As a safeguard, it is vitally important that, at the outset, each Caring Community first establish guidelines for its work. I urge newly formed Caring Communities to enter into a covenantal agreement whereby all participants are clear about the value of and need to respect participatory involvement, the purpose of discussions, the process of discernment, the continuous need for communal reflection, and the avoidance of drawing conclusions prematurely.

While Caring Communities may initiate group reflection, individual participants are also encouraged to engage in more personal or private reflection. The covenantal agreement I recommend must also address the issue of confidentiality. As the group bonds and trust is established, individuals will often bear their souls in the group. People may share very personal information within the dialogue sessions and through their testimonials. Subsequently, it is extremely important that the personal disclosure of participants not be undervalued or trivialized in any way. Respect for confidentiality is paramount because its violation can quite literally be the death of new and very fragile Caring Communities! I am reminded of a sign that often adorns the walls of Twelve Step programs. It reads, "Who you see here, what you hear here, let it stay here so we can come here."

The primary purpose of a Caring Community is to collectively seek wisdom and direction from God. If this is to happen, and it must happen, Caring Communities cannot be places where individual members are found attempting to control or manipulate others. It must also be made patently clear that Caring Communities are not outcome-based. Rather, they seek continuous engagement in ongoing reflective processes. This caution is important because, in viewing the Caring Community as a task group, our propensity will be to draw upon more traditional and familiar behaviors associated with working in organizational structures. It is true that, outside of Caring Communities, we are, in fact, told that the evidence of productivity is specific outcomes and visible work. This is not true for Caring Communities. Other organizations also have a beginning and end time in which tasks are to be completed. This is not true in the case of Caring Communities.

As we take this important look at forming Caring Communities, an additional word of caution is in order. Task groups and/or business meeting sessions always drive their participants toward reaching conclusions that are specifically related to an assigned mission or agenda. This is an extremely comfortable environment and task assignment for many of us. In particular, highly task-oriented individuals or type-A personalities are especially at home in these environments. However, these same individuals may have real difficulty adjusting to a Caring Community where the primary task is the facilitation and nurturing of a community of individuals for the purpose of critique, reflection, and discernment.

As I draw to a close on the discussion of forming Caring Communities, we should mention that, as a result of their reflective practices, some Caring Communities may assume a mission role or other tasks. And while this is an excellent development and benefit, these tasks must not result in the abandonment of ongoing continuous focus on ideas and topics through dialogue that consist of critical review and lead to reflective action.

Finally, Caring Communities occasionally may encounter individuals who resist the process. All individuals must be held accountable to the covenant, including those individuals who insist on conducting business in the traditional styles of our meetings and program formats.

Chapter V

Repairing The Breach Through The Caring Community

○ ○ ○ ○ ○ ○ ○ ○ ○ ○ ○ ○ ○ ○ ○ ○ ○ ○

Your Kingdom has been weighed in the balance and been found wanting.

—Daniel 5:27 (paraphrased)

It is no coincidence that we have learned that when Christ returns, his first stop will be the church (1 Pet. 4:17). This is not a surprise. In fact, this is exactly as it should be. The charge given every clergyperson is clear: bring souls to Christ. It is to be true to the great commission. It is to love our brothers and sisters—God's people—as we love ourselves. The role of the clergy is all of this, with the caveat that the widest possible nets must be cast in order to bring as many souls as possible to Christ. More importantly, these nets must be cast to include all of God's people according to God's will, plan, and purpose and not irrelevant and artificial standards and barriers that separate us from the very people Christ is calling the church. The nets must be cast through programs and experiences that invite and nurture the presence of the Holy Spirit.

I think that the church should be concerned about Christ's return. If the church can be thought of as a "kingdom" that God will examine to determine if it performing as it should, providing for its people as it should, focused on the right things, possessing the correct priorities, then I am sorely afraid it will be found wanting. In the absence of the Caring Community that Christ mandates, this is the only finding that is possible.

I have spoken about the Caring Community that quite literally saved my life and gave me the faith and hope necessary for the journey I am on today. And while I have talked about the Caring Community through a variety of examples, I want to clarity that without the Caring Community, visioning, discernment, and transformation are difficult, if not impossible. It must be the goal of each clergyperson, the laity, and members of the larger community to understand the power that comes through an investment of time, energy, and resources to do the work of building the kingdom of God on Earth ... of returning humanity to a right relationship with the Creator God.

> *Caring communities are "endowed groups" that are bound by common goals which preserve, support, and nurture. They differ from hate groups because they claim and model love and acceptance for all of humanity.*

It is extremely important to understand that the authentic Caring Community is the nemesis of a hate group. While Caring Communities model love and acceptance for every member of the human family, hate groups do not. While Caring Communities welcome the diversity of God's great family of men, women, and children, hate groups look for differences, which they equate with inferiority and inadequacy. Caring Communities see the value of diversity and embrace, celebrate, and support it, while hate groups consider such a celebration as a sure course to their end and supposed superiority.

> *Members of such communities commit time and energy to serve others by offering, supporting, or embracing and educational opportunities, which are framed as essential to human growth and development.*

Members of the Caring Community embrace a general philosophy that "Service is the price you pay for the space you take." Caring Communities can evolve also from service learning projects and volunteerism, where participants form bonds through the affective domain—their hearts.

More importantly, members of the Caring Community look to the past with gratitude for the sacrifices of others. They don't forget where God has brought them from. They know full well that they stand on the shoulders of those who have gone before them. For members of the Caring Community, time is a gift from God that was always meant to be committed to others. It is impossible for members of the Caring Community to compartmentalize religion, family, or education. Where members of the Caring Community are concerned, especially the community's young people, support in all of these areas is a given.

Family within the Caring Community is extended to those who nurture you and hold you accountable. These communities set out to provide a better quality of life for all of its members. The Caring Community transmits their sacred and respected values to future generations by embracing cultural traditions, history, and legacy through storytelling.

The Caring Community was never intended to be biological. It encompasses each and every man and woman of the community who nurtures you. It has always included the senior citizen, who sees everything and reminds you of whose child you are now and how you are expected to behave. The Caring Community is one where wrong is never personal and never someone else's problem. I agree with the cultural expression so often heard within my community and others. The expression is that, "Those who forget the lessons of the past are destined to repeat them." And so history and cultural traditions are enthusiastically embraced and celebrated. Lest the young forget, storytelling is a primary vehicle for sharing values and expectations and, in the Caring Community, is recognized as such and routinely used for the benefit of young and old alike.

They preserve, enable, and prod others to their higher self, an expectation that each generation will build on prior efforts and successes.

In the Caring Community, members feel enormous pride in the accomplishments and successes of their young people. The adults of the Caring Community place enormous value on the lives of those generations that follow them. Therefore, they are protective and always sharing opportunities for growth and development. They are categorically unwilling to watch any subsequent generation fare worse then their predecessors.

It is important to understand that Caring Communities are not restricted to Christians or to the Christian church community. Rather, Caring Communities can be formed within villages, organizations, not-for-profit organizations, corporations, social groups, and ideally, entire communities.

As today's clergy move forward to develop the Caring Community, it is of paramount importance they understand that the results of what happens after they bring congregants and others together must look and sound very different from what is already in place. Critical reflectivity exercises are necessary to empower community teams through the sharing of ideas and open and free participation. Different results will necessitate doing things differently. Moreover, different results will require thinking differently ... thinking outside of the box ... thinking beyond previously held assumptions.

During the era of segregation, communities did not have a choice about the need to bond, collaborate, and work together in harmony. Disenfranchised people understood that only through a Caring Community could they remain whole and intact. So they sought them out, and unlike today, they found Caring Communities ready and anxious to reach out to them. For the disenfranchised, Caring Communities are unions of hope and bridges for transformation and conversion experiences for all of God's people. However, it remains that one of the greatest challenges to churches today is the acceptance of people who are different in culture, appearance, habits, socio-economic standing, and language. Without moving beyond these very superficial barriers, mission outreach programs are hampered before they are ever implemented. Moving beyond superficial acts of community building and bonding may eliminate many conflicts and power dynamics as members get better acquainted and trust is established. The role of the Caring Community is embedded in Christian ethics and the Gospel. We have failed to carry a legacy forward that was our specific responsibility to do so. It seems to me that the community care role our young people are in such dire need of and which is seen in far too few places was lost with the integration movement, the attainment of higher levels of education, and the upward mobility spiral of an identifiable black middle class. Rightly, we wanted and needed to get rid of the disgraceful and demeaning practices and trappings of legalized discrimination. However, we seem to have thrown the baby out with the dirty bath water!

Through the power of transformative leadership, the breach will be repaired. This book serves as a guide for how to move forward toward that end. Admittedly, it exposes some areas of pain and calls all of us on the carpet for the current state of our communities. At the same time, however, it offers clear instructions for where we go from here. Could I have spoken in less harsh words at times? Would you have heard me as clearly? Probably not! The more academic chapters of this book have been very deliberately sandwiched between chapters that speak more directly to the humanity of the reader. The result is a work that is both descriptive and prescriptive. It is a work that has provided instruction to the reader in what is inarguably the most important area of study for true and lasting change in a world that quite literally seems to be "crying out in the wilderness": transformative leadership. Its potential for raising a new kind of leader is enormous, and its implications for broad-based and widespread application are tremendous for church communities, institutions of higher learning, and an unlimited number of workplace environments.

The work of repairing the breach through the development of the Caring Community is really God's work. Through this work of meeting God's people where they are and just as they are, we will find ourselves becoming more and more like God, and our Caring Communities truly being a mirror of God's kingdom on Earth.

The Caring Community
IS

—A journey into our heart and soul

—The lens that guides our faith and awareness

—A conti3nuous experience

—The foundation for our personal and organizational growth

—A safe and nurturing place

—Our hope for the present and future

—Our pathway to kingdom building

—A mirror of God's kingdom

Can You See What Has Not Yet Been Envisioned?

Postlude

The acts of transformation include risk-taking, taking a journey into the unknown, establishing Caring Communities, sharing significant emotional experiences, and of course, having faith in one another.

Caring Communities really drive the process of transformative leadership within every organization. Leaders who serve congregations or any other organizations must be concerned with seeking input and information from their stakeholders by listening to one another, reflecting together, and being open to change. Leaders should be free to dream and claim new realities. Followers should be allowed to challenge and prod. These acts are, in themselves, ways to unravel traditions that may be less useful in today's global society.

Caring Communities take risks because of their sincere willingness to take a new pathway into the unknown. Like the traveler who chose the least beaten path in Frost's classic poem "The Road Less Taken", Caring Communities will see opportunities where others see uncertainty; they will see potential for growth when others see barriers too difficult to overcome; they will welcome responsibilities when others will cross to the other side; they will understand that taking the road less traveled has the greatest potential for making the difference that both time and God demand.

If a community is truly committed to a mission, faithful leaders and their followers must be prepared to take the journey that seems to lead them off the beaten path. This could not be further from the truth, for the journey that must be taken is the same journey our Lord and Savior took. Our call is identical to the call that Jesus issued to Simon and Andrew when he said, "Come, follow me and I will make you fishers of men." Unless we are fishers of men, women, and children, finding them where they are, taking them just as they are, the Caring Community will continue to elude us. None of us can afford to allow that to happen. There's too much to be lost, including our very lives in Christ.

I would certainly be remiss if I did not close by bringing our focus back to the issue of ethics. While I have spoken to this topic, its overarching importance warrants a closing word at the very end of this seminal work.

The work of transformative leadership is very serious business and must be taken as such. There is nothing insignificant about facilitating significant emotional experiences. The right spirit is imperative for both those we would lead on the journey of challenging previously held assumptions and challenging ourselves. How we handle discussions will always say far more about ourselves than it will ever say about those we lead. We must never forget that the work we will engage in is God's work and that to God belongs all of the glory and honor.

It will be very easy to fall into the trap of accepting credit for being used as God's vessel, but we must never place ourselves in such a dangerous position. As the Caring Community becomes a reality, through God's use of our various gifts, the natural inclination is for humans to begin to heap praise our way. Expect it, but don't, under any circumstances, wait for it. The needs that the Caring Community must fill are much too great. There will be no time to rest and wait for the applause that is not ours anyway. There are 1 million young African American males in prison. Who has time to wait? The number one cause of death for African American women between the ages of eighteen and thirty-four is HIV/AIDS. Who has time to wait? Every twenty seconds, a young person drops out of high school, and the overwhelming majority of them are black. Who has time to wait? Homicide is the number one cause of death of black men in America. Who has time to wait? Seventy percent of the African American children are being raised by single women. Who has time to wait? And so the question of ethics is simple enough. We are engaged in doing God's work. It is a work that is mandated by him, and he alone will get the praise. There is so much to do and there is no time to wait.

Our sense of ethics in this matter should keep us on our knees as we pray for guidance and discernment in all matters related to building the Caring Community. The processes of transformation will bring us face to face with the reexamination of assumptions that some clergy have held, as well as their followers. But we are encouraged to support those leaders who employ visionary leadership.

Will we always like what we see and hear? Not likely. Must we remain open to listening? Absolutely! There must be role models for transformative learning, leading, and working to build the Caring Community, and we must stand up to be role models! Finally, we should know that God will hold all of us accountable. However, the responsibility placed on the shoulders of clergypeople is significantly greater. If there is one final question that we as clergypeople and laity should ask ourselves, I think it should be, "Upon his return, how will Christ judge my efforts to build the Caring Community?" Lest we think for one moment that he will not come to us as clergy and laity first, I remind us all of 1 Peter 4:17, which says, "For the time is come that judgment must begin at the house of God; and if it first begin at us, what shall the end be of them that obey not the gospel of God?"

Are you ready for the journey?

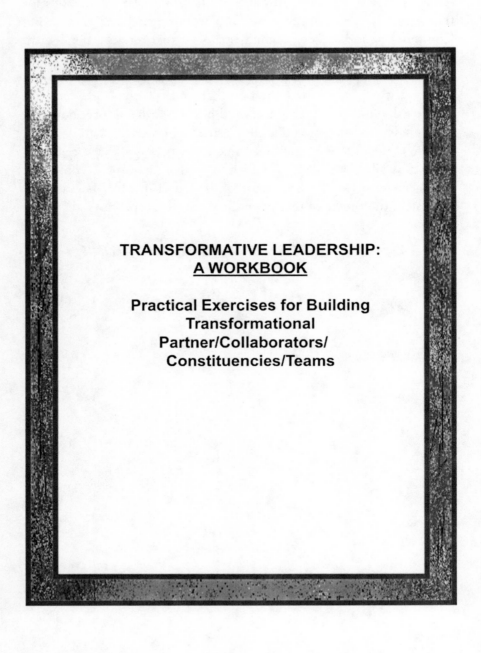

TRANSFORMATIVE LEADERSHIP:
<u>A WORKBOOK</u>

**Practical Exercises for Building
Transformational
Partner/Collaborators/
Constituencies/Teams**

Transformative Leader Inventory Style

Table I enables leaders to test for their dominant style:

TABLE I: Dominant Leadership Style

<u>Instructions</u>: Circle only one response for each numbered leadership/management trait listed below. Select only the **best** trait that describes you. Each trait is worth five points. At the conclusion of your scoring, add up the total number for each column.

The *left column* represents the **transformative leadership** style. If you score sixty points are higher, this is your dominant leadership style. The *middle column* represents the **transactional manager**. If you score sixty points or higher, this is your dominant leadership style. If you receive an equal or close scoring for the left and middle column, you are capable of using both leadership styles.

The *right column* indicates that the individual may be lacking in either the work or life experiences necessary to assess a dominant style at this time.

1.	Optimistic	Hopeful	Unsure
2.	Creative	Focused	Unsure
3.	Visionary	Practical	Unsure
4.	Charismatic	Motivational	Unsure
5.	Boundary Shifter	Boundary Keeper	Unsure
6.	Process Oriented	Task Oriented	Unsure
7.	Problem Poser/Questioner	Problem Solver	Unsure
8.	Intuitive	Logical	Unsure
9.	Risk-Taker	Cautious	Unsure
10.	Transitional	Anchoring	Unsure
11.	Facilitator	Manager	Unsure
12.	Proactive	Reactive	Unsure
13.	Daring	Strong	Unsure
14.	Versatile	Flexible	Unsure
15.	Ambiguity	Clarity	Unsure
	Total Points	**Total Points**	**Total Points**
	( )	( )	( )
	TL Dominant	Transactional Manager	Unsure

TL—Goal is to learn to appreciate the traits of the transactional manager. Without this person, your visions will not materialize, nor will they be institutionalized. These leaders keep the TL grounded and balanced. Communication with the manager is important so he or she understands what you are trying to accomplish and you can offset fears.

TM—Goal is to learn to allow the visionary to dream, to create, and to guide change that can be infused into the organization. This leader is capable of transforming the organization through necessary change. Understand that the new directions may initially disrupt the equilibrium of the organization, but your role is to ensure organizational stability during the change process.

TL-TM Balance—Goal is to help others in the workplace value diversity in leadership styles.

QUESTIONS:

1. As you review your score, what assumptions do you have regarding these traits?

2. Does your leadership style create built-in biases? If so, please describe.

3. What was surprising to you as you assessed your leadership style?

DISCUSSION THEMES

Role of Facilitator

Through the reciprocal sharing of personal stories and experiences, a network of support for the work at hand can be formed. The facilitator gives instructions and monitors the overall process. The community building skills acquired by facilitators usually suggests that they value the concept of Caring Communities. The facilitator's role is to set the tone for building and sustaining an effective and healthy learning community, in support of both personal and group sharing. Facilitators understand that, through the groundwork they lay for the community building process, a safe place will be created for participants that will enable them to dream new visions; challenge each other; explore innovative changes; and critique traditional assumptions and ways of thinking.

Within faith-based organizations, the facilitator may begin this first session with a prayer or a story that moves the participants toward the spiritual domain. The facilitator provides instructions to the gathering about group process, timelines, and intended outcomes. Unfortunately, some participants become disgruntled when they hear the phrase "building community" because they consider it to be a waste of time. It is, therefore, extremely important for the facilitator to clarify that the exercises have great importance and are actually a part of the "real" work of the gathered team. The facilitator would do well to describe this process as laying the foundation for a new house. Through group exercises, a solid foundation is laid for establishing ongoing work that will result in a desirable product.

The facilitator also sets the stage for valuing and respecting each person through ground rules that group members create together and which, subsequently, become a covenant for the group. The facilitator ensures that every person is afforded the same respect, without judgment. It is also important for facilitators to affirm and empower individuals who appear voiceless. In group dialogue sessions, facilitators will want to ensure that each participant is involved and contributes to the process. Toward that end, he or she may decide to use an object such as a rock that can be passed around to each participant who, upon holding it, makes some kind of contribution to the session. The effort to engage all members of the session is to prevent any individuals from dominating the discussion or the process as a whole. Every person's voice and input are important. A second way that facilitators can ensure that no single person or subgroup of people dominant discussions is by establishing time limits as one of the list of ground rules that each participant must follow.

Beginning session:

Unless there is a space limitation, it is best to have the group form a circle so everyone can easily be seen and heard. The circle works best in groups of less than fifteen people. If the group is larger than fifteen people, the facilitator should break the group into smaller discussion circles. Of course, each circle will be involved in the same process.

Regardless of the size of the group, one member should volunteer or be asked to serve as the scribe, and a second member should be asked or volunteer to present highlights to the entire body at the end of the session.

It is desirable to begin with a prayer, devotion, litanies, or general statements about the quality of the group's work. Then the facilitator may move on to select a topic of conversation. This can also be the time when participants start to disclose more personal stories that serve as portals into the spiritual domain. At the conclusion of the session, the facilitator will close by highlighting common themes and new insights gained from the discussion and sharing. Ideally, each person has arrived at an increased awareness of other participants and their various life journeys. The facilitator will announce when the end of the session has arrived and thank everyone. It is best to take a brief break after a couple of hours of work during the first community building session.

Building and Sustaining a Nurturing Community

The following exercises are designed for participants of conferences, meetings, or other group sessions. The purpose of these exercises is to create a culture of respect and a positive tone within the new community. These exercises are also useful as a continuous process for building and sustaining Caring Communities.

GROUP EXERCISES

The following section addresses how to structure conversations that are intended to facilitate the use of critical thinking and perhaps even lead to the affective spiritual domain of learning. This exercise is useful within any leadership context.

First, ask a diverse audience to review television clips or news accounts for the purpose of identifying negative stereotypes regarding dissimilar groups of people through media campaigns, advertisements, and talk shows. Next, ask this audience for specific examples of perceived discrimination or media bias against women, people of color, or older adults.

Second, ask your audience to discuss specific examples from their review. For those audience members who are unable to identify few, if any, examples of stereotypes or discriminatory behavior, place them in a circle. Place a four-sided object (I used luggage) in the middle of the room. Display the following graphics on each side of the object:

(1) Chaotic drawing (red and black coloring) that displays rage
(2) Bouquet of flowers (bright and cheerful)
(3) Happy face
(4) Very sad face

Once the luggage has been placed in the center of the circle, ask each person in the circle to write about what they see and the specific feelings the graphics arouse in them. Tell your group members that whatever they see in the image is actually their "daily reality" and they "never" really stop seeing or experiencing their world or reality differently than what they see when they see the graphics.

For the Chaotic Image:

Suggest to your audience members that each of them, along with eight other people, live in a one-bedroom apartment in Spanish Harlem. You do not always know where your next meal will come from and have experienced not having food to eat because language has been a barrier to locating employment. Your lack of education is another barrier to both a good job and a rewarding career path. Your reality is dim and bleak. Whatever decisions you make are conditioned by what you see each day: hunger, oppression, language barriers, and discrimination. You have had limited support from parents who were also deprived of education and social status. Like you, your parents have had to work at any job they could get just to keep food on the table. You live according to the standards or expectations of your station in life. Your main objective is to stay safe in your neighborhood. You are very fearful for the safety of your children and struggle each day just to make it to the next day.

The Bouquet or Happy Face:

For those who have the bouquet or happy face, the facilitator should say they belong to a power group with lots of resources and support. They are well-educated and even as college students, they did not have to work; they simply enjoyed being a student. Their college days were definitely their salad days. They have been able to gain employment that had led to upward mobility. They are also afforded opportunities for socialization within prestigious social and professional organizations. They live in beautiful homes and have cars and other resources at their disposal. They tend to be happy and satisfied people most of the time. This is the way they see their world each and every day. They refuse to hear about or try to understand the complaints of others. After all, they received their education and have made something of themselves. They refuse to understand why others cannot do as they have done.

The Sad Face:

For those with the sad face, the facilitator should tell them they are depressed most of the time and always see doom and gloom. They question why they were even born and struggle to find even the smallest amount of joy in the world. Everyone else appears to be happy and getting ahead while they spend their time crying over problems and finding fault with others because they feel robbed by the world around them. They are afraid to try new options for fear of failure. They are sick and tired of hearing about the problems affecting minority groups and/or low income people. The sad faces of the world do not want to hear complaints from others because they are too busy focusing on their own problems. If asked to describe their problems, the list would include all of their daily interactions with others, as well as the events of each day. It is possible for these people to be productive; however, they do not keep friends for very long.

Facilitator:

- After you have described these conditions, please share with participants that the seating in the circle allows some of them to see and live between two realities. How does this "conflict" in images make them feel?
- Next, ask them to go back to their original discussion once they really understand how they feel in their assigned reality.
- At the end of this discussion, invite participants to share what they learned, what insights were new, and how they view these various prototypes as they think about making decisions and viewing their paradigms. Ask those who might have resented being a part of the activity whether they can now see through the lens of these other groups.
- Summarize the learning session by focusing on a major purpose of transformative leadership, which is to help individuals understand how they may have their own realities but can sincerely appreciate the perspectives of others. Do participants sense the feelings of others? Are they able to better understand differences in thinking and the lens out of which others screen information?

Hopefully, the facilitator will foster critical reflection and manage to open the lens into the spiritual domain of learning.

FOR CONGREGATIONS

CHURCH REVITALIZATION

Describe the ideal ministry for kingdom building within your own context:

(1)

(2)

(3)

What would you like to see changed?

Develop creative and innovative approaches to your ministry: your outreach as well as your nurturing of members and the community:

(1)

(2)

(3)

Name some ways in which *you* might change—your *ministry* might change:

Moving Your Ideas to Action:

(1) Develop a plan of action for the change that you wish to see in your congregation.

(2) Develop a plan of action for yourself. How will you make a positive difference?

Tell us how you intend to develop support and ownership for the change you seek:

The leader will ask that a covenant statement be developed and monitored by the group.

BIBLE STUDY

There is one particular Bible study exercise that has been useful in assisting churches and their leaders to utilize transformative aspects related to mission and ministry. The exercise is taken from the Book of Acts, where I engage participants in dialogue, with an agreement that everyone is free to share openly and to be heard. All participants are asked to read this entire book and to journal notes and new insights. Then individuals can come ready to share their insights or new ways of interpreting Scripture within the study circle.

Book of Acts

The Book of Acts describes God's purpose for the world and the bringing of the kingdom of God. Bringing in God's kingdom is about *transformation*, which is marked in ACTS by: (1) *conflict*; (2) *diversity*, (3) *inclusiveness*; (4) *recognition that we must be led by the Holy Spirit, and (5) an opening for change to occur in one's thinking*. Basically, the Book of Acts tells us a lot about change and transformation. We also learn that within the transformational model, not everyone will experience change.

This book also has much to say about the importance of relationships and community that is modeled by the disciples. It is my belief that building the faith community and establishing honest relationships allow God's Spirit to be discerned.

According to Suzanne Dietrich in *The Witnessing Community*, the community in the Book of Acts is reflected in three Greek words:

(1) **Proclamation (Kerygma)**—preached and proclaimed message of the church
(2) **Fellowship (Koinonia)**—togetherness, sharing of life based on conviction/loyalty
(3) **Service (Diakonia)**—service of brothers and sisters together, based on mutual goals and obligation

It is important to emphasize that at least two of these Greek words are linked to the Caring Community's transformative process of leading and learning:

(a) *Service*, which is akin to civic engagement and service learning
(b) *Fellowship*, which is akin to learning cohorts, dialogical sessions, and especially the framework for the caring community concept

The Book of Acts describes other essential elements of transformational learning through a linkage between tension and confrontation. This tension is essential for the process of critical thinking. In this biblical account, God encounters opposition from the world in providing a pathway to the kingdom. In the text, we find Jesus rejected by the world, especially by traditional religious leaders. Such rejection is primarily because he challenges and breaks sacred traditions that are entrenched in the paradigms of current leaders and their followers.

The use of the word "argument" appears throughout Acts and shows that one charge that the disciples had was to confront people about their thinking and beliefs.

Example: *And he testified with many other arguments and exhorted them, saying, "Save yourselves from this corrupt generation.* (Acts 2:40)

Group Questions:

(1) Identify how opposition and change in one's mind and heart never ceases in kingdom building?
(2) Within your context, how do you intend to engage in kingdom building? What are the obstacles?
(3) How you do propose to remove obstacles or to create new opportunities?
(4) Do you have gatekeepers of the "old ways?" How will you empower these gatekeepers toward innovation and change? Are you a gatekeeper? What does the Book of Acts say to you?

FACILITATOR TO PARTICIPANTS:

When the disciples announced to others that Jesus was raised from the dead, many, including religious leaders, could not incorporate this belief into their thinking. We know from scriptural account that the religious leaders felt threatened. This was largely because their power was being challenged. The Scripture also states they were jealous (Acts 5:17). Scripture helps us understand that if we are to accept a message from God, we are more times than not required to change in some way. Change requires us getting in touch with our egos and competitiveness with our peers because these things speak more to our power needs than to any desire to draw closer to God in order to learn more about God's messages and direction for the church.

Religious leaders during the time of Jesus' work on earth were not willing to open their mental models and to break traditions that served their power positions so they could journey to a closer relationship with God. Essentially, their need for power, position, and status, along with boundary protection, deterred transformation. As we continue to examine the work of the disciples, especially as they were being condemned by religious leaders, I argue that transformational leadership was essentially derived from the early Christian community and can readily be seen in faith stories, parables, healings, and miracles that were performed to confront traditional mindsets. As evidenced throughout the New Testament, the status quo was continuously challenged by stirring, powerful sermons and the performing of miracles.

There are numerous expressions of the Holy Spirit in the Book of Acts. Please identify scriptures that correspond to the following actions:

(1) People receive the ability to see or hear communication with the Spirit of God
(2) People are sent forth to perform works of God
(3) People exhibit boldness about the word of God
(4) People experience a feeling of comfort when being led by the Holy Spirit
(5) People become increasingly more powerful in ministry and receive increased power in ministry
(6) People yield their will to God's will
(7) People have greater wisdom
(8) There is an increase in people witnessing
(9) The ability to understand for clarity (discernment) comes from God
(10) Hearing the word/listening ability is enhanced

Being led by the Holy Spirit may take us places we might not have imagined. We become instruments of God in truth-telling, challenging, dialogue sessions, and leading the way and bringing change to self and to others based on the Word. We are naturally proactive in the world when God is speaking through our hearts. Transformational leadership processes aid us in hearing different voices, thoughts, and ideas. It creates that space in our mental processes to discern, to vision, and to act.

At the end of this process, I invite participants to write new insights and reflections in a journal. They are asked to come to the next meeting to discuss how their congregations were transformed or seem to be in the process of transformation.

God promises the gift of the *Holy Spirit* to all:

"For the promise is for you, for your children and for all who are far away, everyone whom the Lord our God calls to him."

Creating Space for Reflection
and Innovation

Within church circles and through my participation with adult education professionals, I have utilized group facilitation skills that often resulted in radical transition in outcomes and directions. Following the conclusion of these sessions, individuals would usually pose the question: *"Tell me what process you used that resulted in change?"* To be very frank, during those times, I was not aware of "why" or "how" people were being impacted. Although I was aware of a deviation from traditional thinking to more innovative and, occasionally, radical shifts in thinking and actions, I did not realize that my style of facilitation was the doorway into transformative leadership.

Some years later, I was exposed to a critical pedagogy within the field of adult education. It then became crystal clear that I was actually engaging the process of "problem posing" or problematizing situations to help individuals deviate from traditional views and blocks to their creativity. Problem-posing is an inductive process designed to help individuals and discussion groups back away from traditional ways of problem solving that block them from a more creative or innovative analysis of their assumptions. Problem-posing gives permission to individuals and groups to dream and to explore alternative pathways of decision-making. The process of offering dramatic change in perspectives pushes us away from our traditional perspectives just long enough for new ideas and creativity to emerge.

Several decades ago, while I was working for a church organization, I was assigned a mandate to assist my denomination in "developing congregations for deaf people." All of the administrative leaders assigned to help me meet this goal had perfect hearing. Yet there we were, trying to plan and set program objectives for meetings and strategies to support the needs of deaf, hard of hearing, and cultural deaf (those born deaf) people.

At the first consultation on our assignment, all of the hearing people assumed that our traditional processes and outcomes would work for this particular assignment. Our group of administrators held assumptions about deaf people and their needs that were compatible with our needs. I convened the very first session that included a few deaf people and noticed that everyone appeared satisfied that we had thought to include sign language interpreters. With meeting agenda in hand and with the interpreters ready to translate our conversation for the deaf people who were present, I posed the question: "Since we are trying to empower deaf people, why not have the meetings conducted and facilitated by members of the deaf community? We can then have the signers verbally give the rest of us the information that is being communicated by deaf people?"

In other words, I had problemized the assumption that the meetings would be conducted by hearing people, and those who were deaf would receive the information a few seconds or minutes following our discourse. As I worked to challenge our standard operational style for conducting meetings, the entire room gave me a puzzled look. They questioned me: *"How will this work?"* I responded with another question: "Who do you think should be the chair of this group?" Again, I received a puzzled look. Then I really problematized the discussion: I simply posed to the group that if a deaf person chaired the meeting, might it not make better sense to have reverse interpretation?

They had assumed that a hearing person would chair the sessions so the invited interpreters would carry on their usual communication with deaf people only after the hearing people had completed their dialogue. Here I was presenting a real challenge and from the perspective of many who were present a real problem. I pointed out that my assumption was that a deaf person would chair and conduct the meeting using sign language. Then, those of us who were hearing would experience what most deaf people regularly experience in the hearing society they also call home.

Everyone was puzzled, including the few deaf people and the interpreters. The deaf individuals did not think they could conduct the meeting. As a transformative leader, I naturally wanted to know "Why not"? And I asked them. After encouraging and urging, there was slowly a buy-in for the suggestion that a person who was deaf should lead the discussion. Finally, Lee, one of the deaf people in attendance, agreed to chair the four-year study group. I might add that I was fortunate to be able to observe the leadership development and empowerment of Lee during this time period. Needless to say, those of us whose hearing was not challenged were forced out of our stereotypical thinking and prior assumptions about the abilities and capabilities of hearing impaired and deaf people. Through a confrontation of traditional patterns of acting and thinking, we were able to effectively move away from traditional thinking to far more creative and innovative ways of seeing reality. The process we went through and which is mandated by all Caring Communities is driven by questioning, problem-posing, what ifs, and "dare we not do this differently" attitudes.

FOR DISCUSSION AND REFLECTION

A Gift From Our Founder, Dr. Mary McLeod Bethune
(1875-1955)
Excerpts From Her Last Will and Testament

I leave you love. Love builds. It is positive and helpful.... Our aim must be to create a world of fellowship and justice where no man's skin color or religion is held against him.

I leave you hope. The Negro's growth will be great in the years to come.... Tomorrow, a new Negro, unhindered by race, taboos and shackles, will benefit from more than 330 years of ceaseless striving and struggle. Theirs will be a better world.

I leave you the challenge of developing confidence in one another.... Negro banks, insurance companies and other businesses are examples of successful racial economic enterprises.... Negroes have got to demonstrate still more confidence in each other in business...

I leave you a thirst for education. Knowledge is the prime need of the hour....

I leave you a respect for the uses of power. We live in a world which respects power above all things. Power, intelligently directed, can lead to more freedom. Unwisely directed, it can be a dreadful, destructive force.

I leave you faith. Faith is the first factor in a life devoted to service. Without faith, nothing is possible. With it, nothing is impossible.

I leave you racial dignity. I want Negroes to maintain their human dignity at all costs.... We have given something to the world as a race and for this we are proud and fully conscious of our place in the total picture of mankind's development. We must learn also to share and mix with all men.

I leave you a desire to live harmoniously with your fellow man. We are a minority.... living side by side with a White majority. We must learn to deal with these people positively and on an individual basis.

I leave you finally a responsibility to our young people. Our children must never lose their zeal for building a better world. They must not be discouraged from aspiring toward greatness, for they are to be the leaders of tomorrow....

Faith, courage, brotherhood, dignity, ambition, responsibility—these are needed today as never before.... The Freedom Gates are half ajar. We must pry them fully open.

Invite discussion on Dr. Bethune's Last Will and Testament, which was written in 1953. Is it still relevant for today? If so, in what ways is it relevant? How do you feel about other racial groups being excluded in this will?

LEADERSHIP STYLE—TRANSFORMATIVE
Group Discussion Topic

A transformative leader arrived at his new organization and, when thinking about fundraising, genuinely felt that the present appearance of the building where his office was located would not inspire giving. The building was simply unattractive. His first mistake was that he assumed everyone in his organization thought as he did. Because of this, he understandably forged ahead to improve the appearance of his office as well as workspaces within close proximity. Instead of embracing the new facelift, there was outrage from his constituents. The perception was that the new leader was self-centered and focused on spending the institution's money on himself. Moreover, people he had hoped would view themselves as his partners and embrace the changes instead saw the spending as foolish and even disrespectful of the organization. Sadly, neither the leader nor his transformation partners/collaborators had taken the time to initiate discussions about their expectations or the various assumptions they held about anything, much less the appearance of the areas the new leader felt compelled to change shortly after his arrival.

To transformative leaders, what needs to be done is clear. There is little uncertainly within them about what they are doing or the reasons their specific actions are warranted. However, it can be very difficult for these leaders to understand why anyone would resist what they view as a positive, progressive, and logical change or need for innovation. A striking characteristic of transformative leaders is their propensity to see beyond barriers and obstacles to enormous levels of possibility. Many who have observed transformative leaders doing what they do recount how the leader shared his or her vision that, frankly, appeared to the observers almost impossible to realize. These same people reported being shocked when the visions became reality.

There is no doubt that transformative leaders would benefit from having help viewing change and innovation in the same ways that their transformative partners/collaborators do.

If conflict between partner/collaborators and transformative leaders is to be avoided, effective planning and essential two-way dialogue are imperative. This is the only way to identify needed changes and hopeful outcomes. Accountability to constituency groups means that effective communication and honest feedback are invaluable to help many transformative leaders understand more clearly why others seem to not value change. Traditional leaders do not understand why transformative leaders are constantly changing and "making waves." The reality is that both may be guilty of not having set forth clear accountability goals that will help them understand each other's expectations. It is also important that genuine efforts are made to ensure that partner/collaborators experience an unqualified feeling of joint ownership of both organizational goals and outcomes.

Discussion Questions:

Why do you think that transformative leadership is so difficult to understand?

What insights would you share with both leadership styles? Manager versus visionary leader.

Facilitators may refer to the following discussion for additional guidance.

Neither a Sycophant Be—What Is the Importance of Teams?

Transformative leaders should also surround themselves with leadership team members (collaborators and partners) who will give honest feedback, make suggestions about how to facilitate effective communication, and in general, help them minimize mistakes. Leaders must depend on team members to raise the level of caretaking and fill gaps that impede the development of a Caring Community. Most transformative leaders count on transactional managers to keep them grounded and in harmony with their constituency groups. Although their dominant style will lean toward innovation and visionary leadership, many transformative leaders will also possess certain transactional leadership skills. In either case, effective communication will consistently involve the creation of messages that are purposeful, dialogic, value-centered, ethical, reciprocal, and ongoing.

DISCERNMENT

Because of the decline in church membership, as well as a general lack of revitalization within mainstream churches, transformative leadership, which is capable of fostering acts of the "discerning" process, is a matter that many Christians are concerned about. Yet many of our congregations do not have a clue about how to move into visioning, which is a critical part of church decline. Many church leaders are finding value in the ability of transformative learning techniques to build effective clergy and laity leaders, who are then able to meet the challenge of revitalizing their respective congregations. This paradigm offers a new perspective on how to vision and discern God's movement within individuals for the benefit of outreach mission and ministry.

DIALOGUE QUESTIONS

(1) Describe how you approach the tasks, committee assignments, and other ongoing mandates within your local church?

(2) Do you take the time to allow reflection, individual sharing, and moments to hear God's voice speaking to you about the direction you should take?

(3) How many times do you hear individuals in your organizations reminding others about the "importance" and value of continuing with historical ways of doing business and holding on to traditions?

(4) Describe what happens when new ideas emerge that conflict with tradition?

(5) Can you imagine how discernment is possible within your current meeting practices and processes?

(6) What would you change? Preserve? Why?

COVENANTING PROCESS

In the formation of Caring Communities, it is essential that each member understand expectations and the purpose of their community. Equally important, group members must respect confidentiality and model mutual respect for one another. The covenant serves as a contract or a memorandum of understanding that each member signs at the beginning session.

The covenant serves as a reminder to members who deviate from the purpose and commonly owned norms that are established. While a group may have a set task, the covenant is a reminder that the group must first be bonded for critical reflectivity and transformation to occur.

Step One: A facilitator or designated group member will ensure that some form of devotion takes place to ground individuals in humanistic values of care-taking. The care-taking includes one another, society, and the world at large.

Step Two: The facilitator outlines the purpose of Caring Communities and the importance of entering into covenant with one another.

Step Three: The facilitator leads the group in setting group norms and expectations for individual sharing. This is a very important step as the group determines what intervention is used when any member deviates from the group norms.

Step Four: Confidentiality is a vital part of mutual respect and trust. Information discussed in the group remains there. This action is especially important for individuals who participate in a Caring Community formed by their career organizations so they are not penalized for their beliefs and ideas.

Step Five: Each member of the group executes the covenant by signing a statement of covenant that will include:

(1) Group norms (inclusive of the role of critique of assumptions)
(2) Meeting times and places
(3) Expectations
(4) Mutual respect for one another
(5) Confidentiality
(6) Periodic assessment of progress
(7) Group ownership of outcomes
(8) Individual reflection from journaling between sessions

COVENANT FORM

Individuals understand the following information pertaining to their Caring Community by checking each item listed below:

_____ Purpose of the Community
_____ Requirements/expectations for participation
_____ Confidentiality of information/personal sharing
_____ Periodic assessment and feedback
_____ Respecting differing views
_____ Ability to listen to others without drawing quick conclusions
_____ Importance of individual and group reflection and critique
_____ Ability to give feedback when any member violates group norms and expectations
_____ Commitment to time (respecting start and ending times for sessions)
_____ Receptivity to relinquishing "expert" roles held in other positions and organizations (every participant is equal)
_____ Willingness to build a Caring Community prior to working on tasks or programs

---

I agree to enter into covenant as I participate in developing and sustaining a Caring Community. When I am unable to fulfill this commitment, I will notify the Community.

Signed: Date:

Caring Community Steward

As each person signs, there should be a formal ceremony to highlight the significance of this important stage of community formation.

If an outside facilitator has been utilized to develop the community, it should be clear that the facilitator role can rotate among group members to ensure power dynamics do not enter into the community from an unbalance of authority.

Words like "authority," "individual power," and "expertise" completely disappear if the group expects to seek the wisdom of God through community.

It must also be understood that the reflection that begins in the community continues long after the group dismisses. Therefore, each member is encouraged to maintain reflection journals. As they reach new insights from within or outside of the group, they may share these perspectives.

For faith-based groups, worship and devotions are encouraged during the initial ceremony for forming a Caring Community. Within corporate groups concerned with showing diversity for all religious faiths, humanistic statements that are ground in the ethics of care-taking of society may be utilized.

HOW DO YOU DEAL WITH DIFFICULT PEOPLE WHO CONFRONT THE GOALS OF A CARING COMMUNITY?

While it is assumed that all participants of a caring community share basic humanistic goals of respect and care for one another, occasionally there are individuals who may display nonproductive actions and behavior. Such individuals may be *unable* to participate in a Caring Community. Signs of dysfunctional behaviors may be obvious from the very beginning of the formation of a Caring Community. People who display destructive acts and deeds may need to be dismissed from the Caring Community if they continue to violate the group's covenant. This is why it is so important to launch a Caring Community by adopting group norms, a covenantal agreement, and clear repercussions for those who oppose the purpose, processes, values, and intent of such communities.

Reprimands may be given in a variety of ways as a mechanism to remind all participants of group expectations and appropriate behavior. Such reprimands need to be identified during the initial covenantal agreement. The standards for an effective caring community must be approved and owned by all participants.

Precovenant Discussion:

Prior to developing your group covenant, ask each person to contribute words or phrases that may signal dysfunctional behaviors or other forms of abuse toward a Caring Community. Ensure that your Caring Community covenant includes actions that should occur in the event your caring community encounters difficult and destructive participants.

Characteristics of a Caring Community

Exercise: Ask your organizational leaders to identify what they consider to be ideal characteristics of a Caring Community.

Here are some suggested words or phrases:

- Friendly peers who make you feel comfortable
- Where you can voice your opinion and be heard
- A safe environment without fear of safety
- Nice people
- Trustworthy community
- Expression of concern for others
- Helpful
- God-fearing

References

Burke, K. *A Rhetoric of Motives*. New York: Prentice-Hall, 1996.

Covenant House Newsletter. Fort Lauderdale, FL: Covenant House of Fort Lauderdale, 2004.

Cowman, L.B. *Streams in the Desert*. San Francisco: Zondervan, 1997.

Franklin, K. *Rebirth of Kirk Franklin* [CD]. Inglewood, CA: Gospocentric, 2002.

Freidman, T. *The World is Flat: A Brief History of the Twenty-first Century*. New York: Farrar, Straus and Giroux, 2005.

Johannesen, R.L. "The Emerging Concept of Communication as Dialogue." *Quarterly Journal of Speech* 57 (1971):373-82.

Kimbro, Dennis. *Think and Grow Rich: A Black Choice*. Greenwich, Connecticut: Fawcett, 1992.

King, Jr., M.L. (1962). *Wall Street Journal*.

Long, N. *The Life and Legacy of Mary McLeod Bethune*. Cocoa, FL: The Florida Historical Society, 2004.

Mezirow, J. *Fostering Critical Reflection in Adulthood: A Guide toTransformative and Emancipatory Learning*. San Francisco: CA: Jossey-Bass, 1990.

Pollock, J. *The Apostle Paul*. Colorado Springs, CO: Cook Communications Ministry, 1972.

Preciphs, T.K. *Unpublished Doctoral Dissertation*. Columbia University, Teacher's College, 1989.

Reed, T.K. 1996. A New Understanding of "Followers" as Leaders: Emerging Theory of Civic Leadership. *Journal of Leadership Studies* 3(1).

Walker, A. *Love and Trouble: Stories of Black Women*. Orlando, FL: *Harcourt*, 1974,

LaVergne, TN USA
02 February 2010
171679LV00005B/2/P